1

Exactly As I Remember It

Shane L. Bishop

DEDICATION

This book is dedicated to
My wife, protector and dearest friend
Melissa Anne Bishop.
She is everything to me.

Set Apart
By Michael Gary Harrison

Deep beneath the crust of life
Truth and Way and Love are mined
Spirit-breathed, sweet gems he finds
To speak each week to hearts and minds

Faithful, true, yet son of man
Holy, called, yet from our clan
Righteous, whole, by God's won hand
A fearless lion as heaven planned

Double honor to this one
Blessings on his loving heart
For he doth hear the Word of God
And speaketh rightly, set apart

(Used with permission from A Spark in Darkness)

INTRODUCTION

Growing up in the House of Bishop I learned a lot about timing. For example, the time to sing as loud as you can, attempt to play each of Casey Kasem's *American Top 40* songs on the kazoo and drive my little sister Jill toward insanity was not while we were riding in the car between Illinois and Texas. Dad taught me that one. I have repressed most of the gory details, but I faintly remember flaring nostrils and something coming in hard from the left side. I also learned the time to be hysterically funny, do impressions of Rod Stewart singing Fannie Crosby hymns and have the biggest Double Bubble blowing contest was not in church. Dad taught me that one too. As a very young child, I learned my deportment during morning worship was directly related to my ability to comfortably sit down during lunch. You will read more about that later...

I also learned that the time to stay up all night, watch all the shows my parents wouldn't let me watch (M*A*S*H, Love American Style, Bewitched and what-not), drink a full half gallon of Root Beer and eat dozens of fudgesicles was at Grandma Helen's. Quite unlike my mom, hearing bad words, shows about witches and watching people break various and sundry commandments on television didn't bother Grandma at all. (She would have loved modern cable.) Grandma was undaunted the night I threw up five root beer floats into her toilet or the many nights I suffered from career-ending stomach cramps. Every time I visited her mobile home on Line Street, I would get sick and on my next visit she would have the fridge stocked with soda and ice cream waiting for us to do it all over again! Mom always wanted to link cause and effect. Mom was predictable and boring with her excellent parenting and unwavering insistence I become a functional adult. Grandma had little interest in connecting behaviors to consequences; the time at her ten by fifty-foot mobile mansion was always party time.

There is truly a time for all things but it is always the right time to be moral, honest and ethical. It is always the right time to keep your promises, be a person of integrity and create space to tend your soul. It is always the right time to listen more than you speak, pray about a decision in your life and spread a little sunshine to those around you. As I was thinking about timing, I thought it was about time to finally compile this collection of short stories, slices of life and personal proverbs. It is my hope they will become a literary Box Score attesting to the first five innings of my life, provide some graceful vignettes testifying to the love of God, offer some spiritual insight and make you chuckle just a bit.

When I accepted the call to ministry in 1989, my dad told me, "Tell other people's stories until you get your own." These are my stories. There is nothing here that falls into the category of fiction, though I realize that others who shared the same experiences may recount the stories quite differently. I am sometimes asked if all my stories are true and I reply, "Every story is told…exactly as I remember it."

A Slice of Life

My paternal grandfather's name was Hallan Laverne Bishop. He died before I was born. He named his only son Frederick Laverne Bishop. For some reason, Laverne II dropped the "e" and named his only son Shane Lavern Bishop (that is me). They tell me Laverne used to be a guy or girl's name but then the sitcom "Laverne and Shirley" hit the airwaves on ABC in 1976 and it was all over. In 1984 when my son was born, I felt the pressure of three generations weighing heavily upon me. Then I saw him for the first time. He was screaming his lungs out, had a bluish tint and his head looked like a peanut. When the nurse came in to get the name, Melissa and I responded in unison, "Zechariah Christian Bishop." Sorry Laverne I and Laverne II; Lavern III couldn't pull the trigger; the kid seemed to have enough going against him already.

Harold
(Sumner, Illinois, circa 1994)

Harold killed people in World War II and then worked 30 years in a condom factory. These two life events shaped his personality like an irregular pair of shoes eventually deforms the feet. Harold was my neighbor. I walked by his mobile home each day on my way to and from the parsonage to the Sumner United Methodist Church. I was warned about Harold, "He is a recalcitrant, and curmudgeon old man who doesn't like anybody but especially hates preachers." Harold sat outside in good weather and I cheerfully greeted him every morning and evening. He raised a hand but never spoke. This was our routine and we did it every day. One day, he said, "I heard you like sweet tea." I replied, "That is not exactly right; I like fresh brewed, southern sweet tea where the sugar is melted in while the water is hot." He said, "I can make tea like that. Stop by sometime." I told him I would and walked on to work. (We had been at this for three years; I didn't want to appear easy.) A couple of weeks later I paid Harold a call and he talked about WWII. He spoke of young men who didn't return home, described the face of a female German sniper he had shot out of a tree, described the circumstance resulting in two Purple Hearts and watching his own surgery being performed in the chandelier above him. He also spoke of how badly the church had hurt him as a young man and he cried through most of it. He then turned off the tears, said he didn't need me or the church and I was curtly dismissed. I left a half glass of sweet tea on his table. After that our relationship returned to normal, but I thought a lot about Harold.

One night his wife Edna called me in the early morning hours in a panic, "I can't control Harold; he is having seizures and the ambulance isn't here. Can you come and help me?" When I arrived, Harold was in the restroom with his eyes rolled back in his head, pants hanging at his ankles and was urinating all over the place as he convulsed against the wall. I took a deep breath, waded in and helped Edna. All the while Harold was crying out to God. "God, if you will let me live, I will give my life to you."

The ambulance arrived, strapped Harold to a board and took off for Evansville. I went home and took a really long, really hot shower, threw my clothes in the washing machine and went to bed. A couple of days later, I drove the hour and a half to Evansville and entered Harold's room. He was in pretty bad shape but that did not keep him from literally turning away from me. We sat in silence for several minutes. When Harold saw I wasn't going to leave, he whispered over the oxygen tank, "I meant what I said about giving my life to God; I meant that, but you won't be seeing me in your church. I am going to watch Robert Schuler on television." For some reason, that one really hacked me off and I got about two inches from the tube up Harold's nose. "I have a great idea for you Harold; the next time you are having seizures, peeing all over the restroom, are about three quarter's nuts, why don't you have Edna give Robert Schuler a call? See if he will get out of bed and come over to your house in the middle of night, help your wife care for you and endure your unique physiological rendition of showers of blessing?" I slammed the hospital door behind me and left. It occurred to me this was possibly not a textbook example of pastoral care. There would be no case study.

Harold was released the next week and though he never said a single thing about our hospital conversation, he never missed another worship service at the Sumner United Methodist Church. He sat about midway back and to my right. Edna sat next to him beaming. Harold was alive and in church; her prayers had been answered. About a year later, I received another call from Edna. Harold was dead in his Lazy Boy and she wondered if I would stop by and sit with her until the Coroner arrived. There we sat in three chairs in the tiny living room; Edna, Harold and me. Edna began to cry, "I don't exactly know what you said to Harold in the hospital room but it changed his life." A bit perplexed, I asked, "Did Harold say anything at all about our conversation?" Edna replied, "Not really; he just said you were the first preacher who ever explained things to him in a way he could understand."

Sometimes bad evangelism is better than no evangelism...

Adios and "Gratchets"
(San Pedro Sula, Honduras circa 2005)

When we decided to focus a part of the "around the world" ministry of Christ Church in San Pedro Sula, Honduras, I was excited. My dad had been a part of a mighty movement of God there and the city was in my blood. After making a couple of trips with No Greater Love Ministries, 2006 was our first official Christ Church trip. In the weeks leading up to our departure, my 72 year old Pastor of Visitation Ralph Philippe informed me that he wanted to join the expedition but I was less than enthusiastic. "Ralph you are older than six kinds of dirt and I can't imagine one good thing that could happen." His face turned red, his ears turned purple and he retorted, "I didn't need a mother before I met you and I don't need one now." When I asked if he knew any Spanish he smiled and replied, *Adios* and "*Gratchets*." Perfect. I had a roommate.

About half way through our trip, Marvin and Karen Steinke split us up into a medical mission traveling to Tela on the coast and a construction crew to stay in San Pedro Sula. I opted for the medical mission and encouraged Ralph to come with me. "I am not going to do it. I know how to do carpentry and if I were on the medical mission I would be as useless as you are going to be." We laughed and parted company. While in Tela, I received word that Ralph had fallen off the roof of the church the team was repairing. He was in a comma and had suffered serious head injuries. To make a really long story short, Rev. Ralph eventually died from the injuries he sustained on that trip. Words cannot describe the depths of pain his injury and death brought to Christ Church. Words cannot describe how much I miss him. Every now and then I will run into somebody who knew Ralph and they will inquire if he is still alive. When I respond, "No," they always follow up, "How did he die?" I remember and reply, "He died well.

- Positive thinking is a wonderful thing...just don't confuse it with the Gospel of Jesus Christ.
- Resist the temptation to whine by focusing upon your disdain for whiners.
- God will never ask you to do what He has not equipped you to do.
- You don't reap today what you sow today. If you are sowing good things right now, rest assured good things are coming your way!
- Change always involves loss for someone...good leaders feel this but lead nonetheless…
- I am not sure you can simply throw the Easter Bunny and the Resurrection in a blender, add ice and call it an Easter frappe…
- Jesus' Ascension did not "take Him away" from His church; it assured each of us collectively could know Jesus personally.
- Christianity is something you have to do by the Book.
- The teachings of Jesus Christ fly in the face of common sense...they are most uncommon indeed.
- Converts are made in a minute but the forging of a disciple takes a lifetime.
- We have 'to know' what Jesus said before we can 'do' what Jesus said.

- When God moves powerfully, things get messy. Don't quench the Holy Spirit because of your need for control.
- There is no more lame excuse than "I can't find the time." We all have the exact amount of time.
- Adversity hits at our weakest point; it will make us stronger in time if we do not shrink from it. Run toward the giant.
- Expect attack after times of great spiritual celebration. Satan always wants the ground back he just lost.
- Christianity is a personal relationship with God through Jesus with all of its messiness; it is seldom organized and never a religion.
- When we have done all we can do, the rest is up to God; we are in a wonderful place.
- These days I am more concerned about staying in relationship than always being right. This does not mean I don't want to be right...
- We will never reach anyone for Jesus Christ, if deep in our hearts; we think we are better than them.
- The long-term effect of sin in an individual life is complexity.
- I wonder how many people give up when they are on the very verge of victory?
- Generosity works from a limitless resource perspective, for generous people realize that God is the source.

- Without an understanding of sin, Easter is like celebrating the cure for a disease you didn't know you had...good but not that exciting.
- A holy determination to flourish right where you are is the first step to effective leadership.
- Don't focus on driving out the darkness; focus on getting more light...the light will drive away the darkness.
- You don't "get" the Gospel. The Gospel "gets" you.
- There is this relentless optimism at the heart of Christianity that can be summed up in one word: Resurrection.
- Do the right thing the right way and you will get the right results in the right time.
- Everyone wants to change the world...unless, of course, it requires something of them...
- If you are going to give God all the glory...let Him carry all the stress.
- Sin is often found in the disconnection between our good intentions and our failure to act...
- Had to go to both Lowe's and Home Depot. Different crowds. Same concept...like Methodists and Baptists.

A Slice of Life

This year I turned fifty.
I am not middle-aged.
No one in my family has ever lived to be one hundred.

A Nefarious Shetland
(*Pinckneyville, Illinois, circa 1971*)

When I was about ten, we lived three miles north of
Pinckneyville on Highway 127 in the tiny parsonage of the
Oak Grove Baptist Church. It was 1971 and my father
served as the pastor, worship director, secretary, youth
director, custodian, bus driver and exterminator of the small
country congregation. The house in which we lived has
been moved off the church property about two hundred
yards to the north, but it is still there if you drive by. In
those days, there was a huge, metal fire tower to the south
of the church nestled in a small pine grove. I loved to climb
that thing. From there I could see the world! Every now
and then I would buy a wooden glider airplane from the
Ben Franklin Dime store on the town square, take it to the
top and let her soar! I always imagined it flew for miles
and maybe a kid in Okawville would find it and think God
sent him a free airplane. It was a great life!

We had a dog named Sniffee (he sniffed a lot and I was
very clever with names), a grey-spotted white cat named
Loopy, and two Shetland ponies named Brownie and
Ginger. Brownie was a brown pony (I told you I was clever
with names) and about two hundred years old. In fact, dad
had ridden Brownie when he was a boy. It was her final
offspring, a palomino named Ginger that was my particular
nemesis. This animal was a fire-breathing spitfire with an

18

untamable spirit who refused to be broken by man or boy. It was Ginger who dealt me my first life defeat when I tried to saddle break her and was punished by her fury. When she bucked me off, I would climb back on. When she bucked me off, I climbed back on again. If you are wondering how a human can get consistently bucked off a pony the size of a German shepherd, I want you to know that it is not only possible but likely if you mount a particularly nefarious pony. Finally, her persistence paid off; she broke me, I stopped climbing on and that was the end of it. I don't think this is how stories are supposed to end…it is just the way most stories really do.

I have known a lot of people over the years that have big dreams in their hearts. But after they get "bucked off" a few times, they give up and settle for simply existing when they were created to truly live. Jesus said in John 10:10, "*I have come that they might have life and life abundantly.*" What if we absolutely refused to settle? What if our hopes, dreams and aspirations were put back on-line? Let's start dreaming again. Let's determine that when it comes to becoming the person God created us to be, we will never, ever, ever give up no matter how many times we get bucked off! The fire-breathing Shetland ponies of the world should never be allowed to win. And they won't, as long as we keep climbing back on the saddle.

A Slice of Life

When I was a kid I loved to watch *Mutual of Omaha's Wild Kingdom* which ran from 1963 to 1985. I literally grew up with the show. It starred St. Louis zoo-keeper Marlin Perkins. Back then, animal shows were rated PG, not R like they are today and a lot more was left to the imagination. It always seemed to me the show was disproportionately set in Africa and lions were rock stars. Wildebeests were kind of like bit actors on the old Star Trek; if they managed to get on the transporter at all, they were unlikely to return to the ship. Here was the scene that plays in my mind; a pride of near starving lionesses' approach a massive heard of migrating Wildebeests. (The male lions were normally posing, roaring, preening and resting…mainly resting.) As the herd becomes collectively aware of the lions, it shifts and packs in tightly. Then you see it all unfold from the helicopter; one of the young, sick or old gets separated from the herd. At this point I am screaming at my black and white television set (with tin foil wrapped rabbit ears), "Go back to the herd. Go back." (I always did root for the underdogs or in this case the underbeests). Then you see the pride loop around, offer quick chase, attack the flanks and then one goes for the jugular. At this point they cut away to commercial and the gory details were left to your imagination while they tried to sell you life insurance. Getting too far from the herd is a dangerous enterprise for

Wildebeests in the Serengeti. So is getting too far from the church in a fallen world.

Forgetting to Remember
(Fairview Heights, Illinois, circa 2009)

I had a really bad day. Nothing really went wrong but I couldn't find the hours to accomplish what I needed to do. As the day wore on and deadlines approached, my mood became worse and worse. By late afternoon I had clearly deteriorated from affably ineffective to generally curmudgeoned. I had run my emotional gas tank dry at the office; now I was about to come home with no fuel left in the tank. As I pulled into our driveway and walked into the kitchen, I brought my bad mood along with me (I should have left it at church). It was clear Melissa had enough of the both of us after about three minutes. My daughter Lydia was over and she just stayed out of my way.

As I generally stormed about the house feeling like a caged tiger, I suddenly noticed my baby grandson Maddox in the living room. He was lying on a blanket on the floor and he stopped me in my tracks. I plopped down beside him. He is so cool. He looks like all the other blondes in our tribe, has dimples like me and his hair sticks straight up. One day he is going to learn to switch hit, knock down fifteen-foot jump shots and become a mighty man of God. Suddenly all those things I needed to do didn't seem quite so important anymore. My bad mood just seemed selfish and silly.

As I looked at him, I was reminded of the goodness of God. I thought about how blessed I am to have an incredible wife to share my life, a beautiful family, good health and a great church to serve. How could someone so blessed get so bent out of shape over so little? Sometimes we forget to remember God's blessings. I forgot for a while but Maddox helped me remember.

More Sayings of Rev. Shane

- Be content where God has placed you. Be faithful where God has placed you. There you will find passion, power and peace.
- I have never had a single person tell me their life was better since they quit going to church...
- People thrive when encouraged...
- Take one giant step forward on your faith journey today...then hold your ground. Repeat.
- The worst thing that could happen to a drunk driver in the time of Christ is that they would fall off their camel and hit the sand...
- Blessing is offered at the initiative of God but it is consummated by the obedience of mortals. We must be bless-able to be blessed...
- Thinking about what I want for Valentine's Day...what...did I miss something?
- Bad communicators make simple things complicated...good communicators make complicated things simple.
- Sin will put you in one cage and legalism will put you in another, but a cage is a cage. Jesus came to set us free.
- I hear a lot about bullies these days. I wonder how many churches have tanked because no one would stand up to the "Bully on the Board?"

- Cracker Jack prizes have ceased to be disappointing...they are just pathetic.
- All schools have an occasional good season...having a winning program is something else entirely. Same with churches...
- When you truly believe you don't need to listen to anybody; you are in the most dangerous place in the cosmos.
- Something is always chasing you. Calamity pursues the evil and blessing pursues the righteous.
- Sometimes I wonder how many people religion has kept from Christianity...
- I had an epiphany! The person causing all the pressure I have felt this week is me. I told him to knock it off.
- A good idea sounds as good in thirty days as it did the second you thought of it.
- The fear of the Lord is the antidote to fear.
- If you have not stepped up your spiritual life in the past ten years, you, my friend, are effectively contained.
- Hard to think ahead when the roar of right now is deafening...
- Faith and fear are mutually exclusive realms of existence...
- Faith in a fallen world is like running up a down going escalator...the second you stop moving forward, you are headed the wrong direction.

- I believe God will forgive you every time you fall, but I equally believe God appreciates not having to do it every five minutes.
- When David saw Goliath, he ran toward him because the giant was an opportunity too big to miss!
- Encouragers have the "gift of lift!"
- Spiritual problems must be met with spiritual solutions.
- Personal holiness is Spirit-empowered self-management...
- I am a card-carrying member of the Dairy Queen Blizzard Fan Club...deal with it.
- People want to change the world, not serve on committees.
- Spiritual ground is not hard to take; it is hard to retain.
- Don't try too hard to appear spiritual. If you are actually spiritual, you don't have to try.
- There are few things as utterly hopeful as the promise of a new day.
- Living in a fallen world assures life will seldom be drama free.

Zambora the Gorilla Woman
(*DuQuoin, Illinois, circa 1993*)

There is no better grandfather in the world than Fred
Bishop. He was born for the job. His instincts are uncanny.
No matter what Zec's age, Papa Bishop has been able to
maintain an incredible connection with him. No better
illustration could be offered than what happened last
summer. We traveled to DuQuoin to attend the State Fair
with mom and dad. Melissa and Lydia bought wristbands
so they could ride rides all night free. The rest of us felt
that spinning in tight circles, going upside down and
hurtling about might interrupt our intentions of eating
everything at the fair that was not tied down, living or too
hard to break teeth. After an evening of eating and riding,
we were winding down and walking through the midway.
Melissa and Lydia were attempting to regain equilibrium
and the rest of us were trying not to throw up.

Over the other sounds of the fair, I heard a loud speaker
system stating some pretty miraculous news. Just to our left
was the lair of Zambora the Gorilla Woman. The promise
was clear; for just one American dollar, you could enter the
exhibit and witness the beautiful Zambora transform into a
400-pound gorilla before your very eyes! On the front of
the exhibit were paintings of the beautiful (and scantily
clad) Zambora and of a fierce and mighty Gorilla. The line
for the spectacle primarily consisted of tattooed people
wearing black World Wrestling Federation tee shirts. The

excitement was overwhelming them. I watched them enter like sheep, gladly offer their dollar fleece and disappear from sight. In seconds, an explosion occurred inside the exhibit, the door burst open, smoke poured out and toothless people ran screaming from the gorilla formerly known as Zambora.

After a quick cigarette, Zambora (now changed back into a woman) was out in front again chained to a cage with a Python wrapped around her neck. The announcer was hard at work scaring up another crowd. Melissa and I looked at the gathering people with pity. "Who would possibly waste a buck to see that drivel?" I inquired. The second the sentence emerged from my mouth, I saw them. There in the middle of the line! Sandwiched in between a braless fat woman smoking a cigarette and three skin-headed juvenile delinquents were dad and Zec. They had their eyes firmly glued upon Zambora, American dollars in hand and were enjoying the moment like a man who may never have another one. In minutes they were herded with the others inside. Soon, I heard the explosion and Dad and Zec ran from the smoking exhibit. It was then it occurred to me; Zec has the best grandfather in the world. Every young man should get to go to the fair with someone like Papa Bishop and see Zambora turn into a gorilla all in one night.

A Slice of Life

I received a thing in the mail from AARP.
I got it because I just turned fifty.
They tried to entice me to define myself as old.
No deal.
Not yet.
Their offer was not good enough.
They will have to sweeten the pot.

Church Discipline
(*Fort Worth, Texas, circa 1969*)

Dad is a southpaw. There are two files in my memory that
verify this fact. One concerns the fact I could never use his
baseball glove. I could catch with it but I always threw like
a girl. (These days girls throw really well, so I have no idea
what I threw like.) The other concerns the position in
which I was held one fateful Sunday morning in Texas to
receive the discipline of the Lord.

It was 1969. I was seven years old. The *Miracle Mets*
would win the World Series, the world was going crazy and
the Jesus Movement was just beginning to trickle into the
Bible belt from the coasts. Dad pastored a tiny Southern
Baptist church outside Ft. Worth, Texas, where he also
attended seminary full-time and worked 40 hours a week
stocking produce at the local Piggly Wiggly. It was Sunday
morning and the hymn selection was *Count Your Blessings*.
As we began to sing something incredible happened; I
interpreted it to be miraculous. A charismatic impulse fell
upon me, though it apparently missed the rest of the
congregation. (Not Baptist bashing here, it can happen to
anybody.) Compelled beyond any mortal effort to resist, I
jumped to a standing position on the top of my pew while
the congregation remained seated. With great grace, poise
and beauty, I began to count my blessings as I turned in 360
degree rotations. The jig began with one finger jutting into
the air and with each rotation I would add an additional

finger. Though I was certain the rest of the congregation was richly blessed by the fact I had just invented Liturgical Dance, my dad apparently was not (being a fundamentalist and all). Somewhere between my fifth and sixth blessing (while my back was momentarily turned to the pulpit), something most unfortunate occurred. Dad darted from the pulpit, literally snatched me from the pew, tucked me under his left arm like a football and shot down the aisle and out the back like a running back rambling toward the End Zone. The congregation kept on singing.

When we exited the sanctuary, he spun me from his left to his right side and began inflicting the discipline of the Lord upon my scrawny backside. Unknowingly, the congregation continued to sing, *Count your blessings...**Smack**...Name them one by one...**Smack**...Count your blessings see what God hath done...**Smack**.* (As to whether I was an inadvertent participant in the invention of percussion in worship is the topic of another story.) After a brief and unbridled flurry of open-handed instruction, he stood me on my feet, glared at me and ushered me into the church like a police officer ushers a convicted felon from a courtroom. The *cutting-edge* boy prophet of moments before was now paraded before the fickle assembly in absolute humiliation and returned to my mother on the front row. (Who was no doubt enjoying an escapist fantasy that I was the neighbor's kid and she had never seen me before.) Dad summarily returned to the pulpit, rechanneled his energy and preached a rather fiery sermon.

31

As I look back, that day taught me two lessons I will never forget. First, those on the cutting edge are often misunderstood and two…the discipline of the Lord comes swiftly and from the left side.

A Slice of Life

When I was a kid we sang out of hymnals. If you are not old, a hymnal was a collection of four or five hundred songs, prayers and Psalms that churches used before Jumbotrons got saved.

A Bible Story About a Snake
(Louisville, Illinois, circa 1984)

In the summer of 1984 Melissa and I moved to Louisville, Illinois, and rented a house in the country from Herb Bible. I had just graduated from college at SIU-C and was contracted to teach junior high Social Studies in the North Clay District. Herb was a member of the Methodist church and the school board. The house we rented had to be about 750 square feet, but it was palatial compared to the 50-foot mobile home we had lived in during the past year. I only made about $14,000 a year, but it was a fortune compared with the nothing I received for student teaching. Rent was $150 per month. The house was located about a mile and a half out of town just beyond the Little Wabash River. It was surrounded by farming fields and sat on about a quarter of an acre along the Sailor Springs Road. As Herb was showing us the exterior of the home, a large snake slid in from the Milo field and caught Herb's eye. Not even taking a breath from our conversation, he casually drifted over to the snake, grabbed its tail and cracked it like a bull whip. The snake's head violently jerked and somewhere between the subject and verb of a single sentence, a dead three-and-a-half foot snake was being tossed in helicopter fashion back into the field.

Herb never took a breath, acknowledged the snake or mentioned this somewhat traumatic event (especially for the

34

snake) to us. There was no need to relive the experience for Herb, paint snake scenes on a cave wall or take a photo for the Clay County paper. There are snakes in that part of the state and this one was now dead because it was not where Herb Bible wanted it to be. Herb Bible was not unafraid of snakes and any snake with a lick of sense should have been afraid of Herb Bible! I wonder sometimes if we don't overreact to the life-snakes that slither into our paths from time to time. We tend to panic, yell, search for a bazooka or call 911. We stop what we are doing and give the snake 100% of our attention. Herb just killed the snake. Herb didn't think about it twice. If I killed a snake, I would take a picture of it with my cell phone and tell the story over and over. The snake would get bigger with each telling.

Satan is introduced to the readers of the Bible in Genesis as a snake. He showed up where he didn't belong and Adam and Eve just let him hiss. The next time Satan pops up his ugly head in your life, take the Herb Bible approach. Don't panic... just kill the snake. When the snake is dead, don't take it to the taxidermist or make it the subject of your every conversation, just keep on serving Jesus. Christians should never be afraid of snakes...we need to make snakes afraid of us.

More Sayings of Rev. Shane

- Want to do something radical today? Pray for your enemies!
- We don't forgive to let those who hurt us off the hook...we forgive to keep bitterness from destroying us.
- Pray for your enemies. Not that they will be changed to become more like us, but that you will be changed to become more like God.
- Saints and artists struggle to live in this world because they instinctively know they do not belong here...
- We so often pray that God will change our circumstances when we should be praying that God will change us.
- So you have a lousy attitude... How is that working for you?
- Ambition confuses position with purpose...not all worthwhile things move up and to the right.
- As we make the effort to get the Word of God inside our hearts and minds, God provides the power to live according to that revelation...
- Prayer in desperate times forces us beyond the rhetoric of our faith.
- God's purpose for our lives is often thwarted by our own ambitions...

- You and I are either works in progress or suffering from a work in progress stoppage. None of us are finished products.
- A lot of Christians have been spiritual infants for years. They are saved but they really don't want a lot of additional information.
- If you don't think God has specific opinions on things, you have never read Leviticus.
- Peace is not the absence of conflict. It is the presence of God.
- Worship. Serve. Repeat.
- God is not interested in the shortest distance between two points; God is interested in the relationship along the way.
- Evangelism is most difficult for those unsure of what they believe...
- Why is it that updating to newer technology always means things I used to know how to work, I don't know how to work anymore?
- Monday Theme: Taking Care of Business. Feel like I died and went to a Bachman Turner Overdrive song...
- Like the wise men and shepherds, by freely offering our unique gifts to Christ, we play a role in salvation history!
- I would like to state for the record that I preach both steroid and performance enhancing drug free…
- When you finally understand that God wants good for you; it changes everything!

- When you look for daily opportunities to us used by God, each day becomes an adventure!
- Having a great attitude does not guarantee a great day; but it will up your odds exponentially!
- Believe none of what you hear and half of what you see...
- Most of what people think they know about the wise men is from a song published in the Civil War called "We Three Kings."
- US American Christmas is essentially two stories; each with their own storylines, characters and traditions. Santa and Jesus. Parse or blend?
- To the tune of "Piano Man." "It's 3:31 on a Saturday and I'm writing sermons again..."
- There is nothing more difficult or essential than having to learn to work differently...
- Pastoring, preaching and leading are distinct skill sets. Few if any, are equally gifted in all three.
- I have developed a disease called DIS (Drama Intolerance Syndrome). It is raging out of control right now...no hope for a cure.
- Think about the life you want to have in five years. Are the decisions you are making today taking you toward that life? Repeat question tomorrow.

Praise-a-Thons
(Herrin, Illinois, circa 1988)

For a while in the late 80's, dad was active in Christian
television. Active in the same sense piranha are active
when they encounter meat. It was really a pretty good fit.
Television loves larger than life personalities and Fred
Bishop is larger than several lives. Dad loves to learn new
things and enjoyed getting to know the old pros from the
Christian television circuit who took time to show him the
ropes. For a while it seemed we could not turn on the
television without seeing dad. He did talk shows, he did
remotes, he did panels and he did shorts. When we would
go to the mall, people would stop him and ask if he was the
guy on television. It is not a difficult thing to be a celebrity
in Southern Illinois. Like so many others, I watched, but
not because I enjoyed the programming; I watched to keep
an eye out for my dad. Excitement often gets the best of
him.

Once a year the regional station held a Praise-a-Thon. A
Praise-a-Thon is like a telethon, only saved. For this event
national heavyweights would come to preach, croon and
testify for the purpose of raising the station's annual budget.
My dad was a Praise-a-Thon machine. When money would
roll in, it seemed to crank up his already heavily cranked
metabolism. He would get downright giddy. At these times
he would lose his perspective. Once he offered to

personally deliver his hat to the next person to pledge. He and mom had to drive to Cape Girardeau to deliver the hat.

One year while I was watching the Praise-a-Thon, money was coming in slowly. Impulsively, dad decided to earn some of that money he wasn't being paid. Dad decided that for the next thirty minutes he would match the financial pledges of all callers to the station. I began to panic. Dad had no real money and I could imagine some millionaire calling in and pledging a few hundred thousand and hurtling dad to debt and disgrace. I did what any good son would. I called the station. When they asked for my pledge, I informed them I was not calling to pledge. I was Shane Bishop, Fred Bishop's son, my father had gone insane and I was calling to tie up the lines. I would neither pledge nor hang up. When they hung up on me, I immediately called back. The damage was manageable.

For years I couldn't understand how dad could so lose his mind...then I came to Christ Church. We began to hold Capital Campaigns and Melissa and I began to give more than we could have ever imagined. As we gave, God gave back to us and enabled us to give more. It is a wonderful thing to get caught up in something bigger than you are. I am convinced true life happens at the precise point you become consumed in the stuff of God. Dad learned this long ago.

A Slice of Life

I often notice that people tend to shy away from church when things are going bad for them. They seem to feel that God accepts them when they are doing well but is less than enthusiastic about them when they are stumbling, doubting or struggling. Sunday night my grandson Maddox ran to me after church and jumped into my arms. They did water games at Bible School and he was literally drenched from head to toe. It did not occur to him for one second that Papa would not want to hold him just because he was soaking wet (and Papa had on a *dry clean only* suit). We should run to God with such confidence in His love for us. Run to Him...His arms will be wide open!

You're Getting Warmer
(*Sunfield, Illinois, circa 1973*)

When I was a kid, our extended family gathered at my Aunt
Halene's house on Easter afternoon in Sunfield, Illinois.
We were dressed in our Sunday best. While we children
were dispensed baskets filled with fake grass, dad and my
uncles hid a cosmos of dyed, hard-boiled eggs at my Aunt
Floss' house just down the blacktop (the last house before
you got to the lake). When the signal was given, all eleven
of us ran a quarter of a mile down the road and began our
frantic search. At first the picking was easy; each poorly
concealed egg was summarily plucked or left for the little
kids. Then it got a bit tougher and finally nothing obvious
remained. It was in this final stage of searching around
propane tanks, in the pipes of the clothes lines and out
buildings that we would annually find a handful of the most
rank, sulfuric smelling eggs you have ever beheld, left over
from the year before.

In addition to the real eggs, there was one plastic egg with
the name of each child in our extended family written upon
it. You could only pick up the plastic egg with your name
and inside it was a silver dollar! In those days a US
American dollar could buy you one Frosty Root Beer in a
glass bottle, a Baby Ruth bar and six packs of Topps
baseball cards…and still leave you a dime to put in the
offering plate. These individualized eggs were hidden in

places whose difficulty factor was proportionate to our age. A three-year-old's egg was lying on the ground by a tree but a twelve-year-old's egg might be concealed in the rafters of the front porch. It seemed every year I failed to quickly locate my special egg; after quizzing our fellow cousins as to whether they had seen it, I would turn to the adults for hints. With wide eyes, I would move in a direction and Uncle Robert or Uncle Mervin would tell me if I was "warm" or "cold" until I zeroed in. "Warm, warmer, hot, hotter, you are on fire!" Found it!

Many spend their lives searching for something they believe to be out there, but can't quite seem to find. Songwriter Keith Green penned, *"All my life I've been searching for that crazy missing part."* Jesus said if we are asking the right questions, we *will* find answers. Jesus said in Matthew 6:33 that if we keep looking for the right things, we *will* find them! Jesus said if we are (knock, knock) knocking on heaven's door, the door *will* be opened. Perhaps that is what the church does as we endeavor to "connect people with Jesus Christ;" we let people know when they are "warm" or "cold" in their search for things like forgiveness, healing, faith, hope and love. I pray that in our search for things most important this Easter, we will get warm and warmer, hot and hotter until we find…Jesus! And when we find Jesus, we have found everything!

More Sayings of Rev. Shane

- When the kids are all throwing up their corn dogs, slow down the Scrambler...
- Every really cool thing that happens in the Bible occurs when you get some Holy Ghost flying around...
- Look at your present challenge as an opportunity for God to be glorified!
- God is not a D.J. Prayer is not a request line...
- Question the US American holiday template.
- Watching Dave Ramsey...not going to budget but did buy a blue shirt...in cash.
- Christmas is not about unlikely things occurring...it is about impossible things occurring.
- When it comes to inviting, churches should think less in terms of marketing and more in terms of equipping...
- John the Baptist was a guy who missed a turn somewhere between Zephaniah and Haggai and ended up in the wrong testament.
- Think significance rather than success...
- Thirty five years of competitive softball have taught me that the only two things I can control in life are effort and attitude...
- Multitasking is a bad idea if you can't mono-task effectively...

- Never assume that the e-mail you sent was received...if it is important, follow it up with a phone call to make sure.
- Though there is no place like home, there is also no place like a pristine Mexican beach and an all you can eat seafood buffet either...
- Never turn a blessing into an idol...only Christ should sit in the center of our hearts.
- Feel. Pray. Act.
- Headed the right direction? Then hold course!
- Don't let negative people infect you with their disease...
- Garbage in/Garbage out. Guard your mind.
- If salvation is God's gift to the sinner, peace is God's gift to the saint.
- We are a bit peculiar with justice and grace. Justice is what we want for others. Grace is what we want for ourselves.
- Prayer must not be an attempt to lobby God to see things our way; it is a plea that we can learn to see things God's way.
- You should always promise less than you know you can deliver...it is not a question of faith; it is a question of credibility.
- "Almighty God, please allow me to live in such a way today that I call attention to you and not myself!"
- You can't live forward looking back...

- The US American idea that leaders are not, and should not be expected to be role models is both a modern invention and a stupid one...
- Faith is a relentless belief that regardless of your circumstances, your best days are ahead of you!
- What I never want to do as a theologian is take the sins I am least dispositioned to commit, and make them the worst...
- A bad day today can mean a great day tomorrow if you face your challenges head on...
- Leadership is most often required at the precise moments I least want to lead...
- If we are to truly be the body of Christ, Christian people stand in desperate need of one another.
- It is the presence of the Spirit of God that makes a church a church.
- The USAmerican church must gain a sense of holiness among its leaders... devoid of the bitter aftertaste of legalism.
- Update your publicity photo often and don't make it look too good. You don't want people to be disappointed when they see you.
- Amazing how "light" days have a way of filling themselves up with heavier things...

A Lesson from the Kentucky Derby
(Louisville, Kentucky, circa 1985)

I attended a No Greater Love Ministries evangelistic outreach to the Kentucky Derby in the mid-80's. The idea was that as the crowds entered Churchill Downs, we would hoist big Gospel signs, hand out Gospel tracts and sing to them, then do the same as they exited. I was with a small group working the front gate where a friend handed a Gospel tract called "The Big Question" to a drunk and shirtless man in his late twenties. This guy, sporting a few bad tattoos (I hope he wasn't charged full price) in the days before everyone had tattoos, had a crazed look in his eye.

This young man took the tract, stared our group down and summarily ate it. It went well for him at first, but as he chewed and began to experience the full flavor of paper and ink in his mouth, he slowed down. It was clear to me at this point that this was now the best witnessing trip in which I had ever participated. There was a decent-sized crowd watching by this time and we were all wondering how it would go. He was looking about like those guys do on the Food Channel when they are three quarters of the way through a five-pound hamburger. Right when I would have bet that he was going to spit the whole thing out, he reached deep within, conjured up some spit and with a Herculean effort swallowed. Upon the accomplishment of this feat, he looked at me defiantly with anger in his eyes. It was clear I needed to say something to him; I prayed for wisdom how to properly respond, looked him straight in the eyes and said, "Now it's going to be two or three days before you can read your tract." I learned that day not every invitation to Christ will be immediately received well; sometimes it takes two or three days for people to really get it.

A Slice of Life

Do you ever get this feeling during meetings that your life
is being stolen?
You just sit there stranded and dangling on the
sheer rock face of Stupid Mountain.
This is time you will never get back.
There will be a time later in life when you want those hours
returned to you, but they will not be returned even though
you have a receipt.
They are currency you have already spent.
I don't go to many meetings anymore…
Can't afford it.

A Men's Breakfast
(Manchester, Georgia, circa 1989)

It was the winter of 1991. We were in the fellowship hall of
the St. James United Methodist Church in Manchester,
Georgia. It was a Saturday morning and 10 elderly men
gathered with my five-year-old son and me for a men's
breakfast. We ate and the official business meeting began
when the gavel pounded without prayer, devotion or
fanfare. Today's topic, "Why does no one come to our
men's breakfasts?" When Mr. Roy Gilson asked for
possible explanations, my son Zec's hand went immediately
up. Roy smiled and ignored him and called on a more
predictable attendee who suggested that we needed better
food. There was not an argument on that one from me. Our
breakfast of really greasy eggs, soggy bacon and instant
grits served with orange juice clearly extracted from
diseased trees somewhere in Minnesota was not great. Our
treasurer suggested a different day or time and a most
irregular member suggested we should only hold breakfasts
in the winter as not to interfere with his golf game. I was
thinking there is only one month a year in Georgia when
you can't play golf and the idea of an annual January
breakfast was gaining serious traction with me, but all the
while Zec's little hand was in the air waving. Finally, Roy
winked at me and called on Zec. Zec was clearly glad to
have the floor, and being a recent graduate of Miss Moore's
kindergarten class, was full of ideas and confidence. In a
high voice defined by his newly crafted southern accent,

Zec said, "Mr. Roy, I know why nobody comes to these breakfasts or your meetings." There was a pause. Roy said, "Why is that Zec?" Zec replied, "Because you all don't do nothing." Zec was beaming at his now articulated revelation. Mr. Roy frowned at me, grabbed his gavel, abruptly adjourned the meeting, got in his truck and went home. All the guys were still laughing on the way out of the church and each went out of their way to thank Zec for coming to breakfast. Many reported it to be the finest men's meeting they had ever had at St. James. Zec was exactly right. They really didn't "do nothing" at all.

Maddox
(*Fairview Heights, Illinois, circa 2011*)

One Sunday evening after I wrapped up 6:00 church, I was
headed to the car to scare up a late supper. Melissa was
already waiting on me, but I noticed that my daughter Lydia
and her family were still in the sanctuary talking to some
friends. Since I never pass up an opportunity to see my
grandchildren, I took the southbound exit ramp and called
for my grandson Maddox. The sight of Papa sent a twinkle
into his eye; he ran to me and I scooped him up in my arms.
Maddox is two years old and he loves church! He loves his
Puggles class at AWANA (particularly snacks), he loves to
play on the playground, he loves to run in the gym but he
really, really, really LOVES the drums on the sanctuary
stage. On Sundays when the music stops, Maddox yells,
"More!" and is inconsolable when the drummer quits
playing. Now in my arms, Maddox said, "Drums" and we
walked to the stage to get a better look at the drum set.
After a minute or two, it became clear that Maddox had
more time than I did. I knew Melissa was waiting for me,
so I took his suddenly unhappy self ,back to my son-in-law
Ryan, knowing there was an outside chance that the scene
Maddox was about to cause could in some small way be my
fault.

Sensing he was being "returned to sender," Maddox
desperately said, "More Papa" and hugged me with a death
grip but Papa had to go. I gave Maddox to his father in

"full tantrum" mode, complete with dinosaur-type screeching, arched back and kicking hands and feet. Ryan smiled at his son, held him out at a ninety degree angle so he wouldn't hurt himself and playfully said, "Buddy, I love you enough for both of us."

So often when we don't understand God's will, timing, ways or provisions for our lives, we act like a two year old and throw a tantrum before our Creator. We are mad at this God who we declare to be "Good all the Time" because God doesn't seem very good or fair or just at the moment. And yet, rather than reject us, God reaches out His arms, makes sure we don't hurt ourselves and gently says, "I love you enough for both of us."

You Are Simply Killing Me with These Sayings of Rev. Shane

- Trendy is not a synonym of relevant...
- Some of the most unchristian things ever to happen on this planet have been done in the name of Christ. It is inexcusable.
- When religion occludes faith; it moves from an anachronistic thing to a dangerous thing.
- Jesus was always asking people to give up their religion and become a disciple...
- Old athletes won't practice unless there is a game coming up. May there always be games!
- Evangelism is messy work...effective evangelism is messier still.
- More people are just one invitation away from attending church than you might imagine...let that one invitation be yours!
- No matter your vocation...I assure you that you are in the people business...
- Worship announcements are ecclesiastical kudzu; if you don't keep them cut back, they will take over.
- How we think will either become the catalyst or the ceiling to anything we will ever accomplish...
- Tornado warnings? The perfect time to clean your basement!
- Christian ministry must be rooted in love; not duty, guilt or obligation.

- Leaders create the future in which their followers will live...
- Churches that are plateaued often seem bunched up just below the 100, 200, 400, 750 or 1,200 worship attendance marks...
- Treat someone well today who could never do anything for you...it feels...well...Christian.
- I think "nothing personal" is one of the truly boneheaded responses of all time. Everything is personal.
- I once tried out for the Phillies...they were not highly interested in my services. Said they were trying to build a good team...
- If God has called you to Christian ministry, never forget you are in the people business. Otherwise you are just in business.
- All systems are designed to produce what they produce, not what you hoped they would produce. Don't like your outcomes? Change inputs.
- The task of the new Christian is to replace evil with good, but the task of the mature Christian is to replace the good with the best...
- It is always a good day to get smarter...
- Laughter outside my office door is a delightful sound on days I don't have time to come up for air...hope to join in very soon.
- Life blowing up? Get back to the basics.

- Had the St. Louis Cardinals informed me in advance this would be a big game tonight, I would have cleared my schedule.
- Healthy things grow. Growth demands change. Change causes discontinuity. How we deal with discontinuity determines health.
- We are all full of something and we all leak...
- Critics abound in great numbers. I would trade one effective Christian for the lot...
- At church many are able to be, for a short time, the person they truly wish they were all the time.
- We don't know who we truly are until we are exposed to pressure. Give that self to God as freely as you do the Sunday morning version.
- To increase interest in the clergy as a vocation for young persons, I am advocating both clergy action figures and trading cards.

Taking Swings
(*Pinckneyville, Illinois, circa 1970*)

I will never forget my first at bat in Little League. As I stood in the batter's box, my mind was in a frenzy. "Keep your eye on the ball, back arm up, weight on the back foot, swing level and don't back out." Donnie Miller had taught me these things; though he was but a year older than me, he was at least one hundred times the better ball player. Donnie was Johnny Bench and I was Bob Uecker, but he liked me and I was grateful for his friendship. Under his tutelage I had mentally prepared for every possible scenario, except for what happencd.

The first pitch I faced in organized baseball was hurled by a monster from Tamaroa named Billy Ray Johnson. He had a full beard and drove a truck to the game. No mean accomplishment for a seven year old. Warming up he threw heat- seeking missiles. Quite tragically, he had no real idea where the ball was going when it left his hand. Some of his pitches hit the catcher's mitt; most hit the catcher and careened in various directions, but a few were nowhere near the plate and bit into the screen backstop. It was precisely those erratic pitches that most concerned me.

"Batter up!" I dug into the batter's box. Billy Ray went into his windup, reared back and threw an inside high heater honing in upon my head. There was no movement in my body whatsoever; like a deer in the headlights, I froze, closed my eyes, didn't so much as turn my head as the ball hit me squarely in the mouth. In return for getting hit in the mouth, the umpire awarded me first base. As the blood trickled down my mouth, I swore I would never be hit by a baseball again. It was a survival instinct that punctured my psyche and in the precise moment in time when Sigmund Freud met Willie Mays, Freud clearly won. If I could not thrive…I would survive. To aid me in this endeavor, I developed a batting style that practically guaranteed success. When the pitcher was winding up, I would dig into the batter's box and crowd the plate (thus feigning courage). When he was ready to throw, I would leap backwards about three feet, close my eyes and swing the bat in midair (thus establishing cowardice). It turns out that this method was most successful. I was not hit by a pitch for three years! Unfortunately for my teammates and coaches, I did not so much as hit a foul tip in those years but all great plans have a downside. I could live with the humiliation because I could *live!* My fourth year in Little League, my coach told me I could really be a good player if I would hang in there. He explained if my eyes were kept on the ball, I could hit a good pitch and most likely avoid a bad one. He taught me how to get hit by turning my body away from the ball. The advice took me from the worst ballplayer on the planet to a halfway decent one overnight. It is amazing what keeping your eye on the ball can do for you. I wonder how many people live in fear of the ball? They are afraid, so they shift the objective of the game from getting a hit to not getting hit, from loving to not getting hurt and from a life of passionate ministry to a life of punching a clock. Jesus said in John 10:10, "I have come that you might have life abundantly!" I encourage you in this season to push past your fears, keep your eye on the ball and pursue your dreams for an incredible marriage and a family life that honors God. Don't settle for being anything less than you were created to be! And to watch out for bearded seven year olds....

Another Story About Taking Swings
(*Robinson, Illinois, circa 1995*)

Some years ago some guys from my Sumner church formed a softball team and challenged the inmates of the Robinson Correctional Center to a softball game every now and then. We didn't really practice but hoped God would give us a break on the "good hearts and trying to reach out" clause. Knowing it would be an away game, we truly hoped God would use us to be His ambassadors to the inmates and rejoiced that our tax dollars were used to prepare the field for play. When we arrived at the prison, it was a bit unnerving. They reviewed our roster to make sure only the approved players were with us; we were searched and our gloves, bats and softballs were X-rayed. As we walked toward the outdoor commons, I saw a sign that read, "In case of gunshots, fall to the ground." I thought about hitting the ground now and beating the rush. Hundreds of prisoners filled the bleachers, surrounded the diamond and the game began. Guards watched warily from the turrets. I could see their rifles.

While running the bases, I struck up a conversation with their third sacker, a guy about my age they called "Deuce." I discovered we had played baseball against one another in college. I asked, "How did you end up here?" His story was a short one. "We had a few beers one night and a cop stopped us. I got mouthy; he got belligerent and I hit him.

One stupid swing cost me four years of my life." It seems Deuce had sowed the wind and reaped the whirlwind. I had so much more I wanted to ask him, but Jim Baker connected with a line drive to the gap and I trotted home.

On a positive note, I played well and their coach told me that if I ever hit hard times, they would have a spot for me on their ball club. I guess I have that going for me. It is amazing how much difference one good or one bad swing can make in a life. Everything we do matters…make sure you are swinging for the right things.

- I have noted through the years that the people rocking the boat are seldom the folks who are rowing it.
- I had a wonderful week yesterday...
- If you don't plan to give people room to create, don't hire creative people.
- Cast a great vision, find great people for your team and turn them loose to accomplish great things...
- If today looks like a bad day, turn it into a terrible day and do every unpleasant thing you have been putting off for weeks.
- Last Thursday in our softball game, someone yelled "anywhere" when I was batting. Better than the "no wheels" someone yelled when I came up the week before...
- Any purported Gospel with "try harder" at its root fails to be a Gospel at all...
- When we choose to forgive rather than become bitter, help rather than judge and act rather than walk away, we sow seeds of life...
- Being an authentic Christian has far less to do with being absolutely perfect than it has to do with being absolutely God's.
- The witness of an authentic and stubborn faith that holds in the hurricane is the best testimony we have to offer this world.

- Enthusiasm is contagious! Find something truly worth doing today and get excited about it; others will line up to join your party!
- Leaders were God's idea; issues with authority are something humanity came up with after the fall.
- People with lousy attitudes should at least fake it...
- Go out of your way to encourage people today...everyone will win.
- Words like authentic and relevant are far better ways to think about worship services than words like traditional and contemporary...
- A great attitude is a choice, not a disposition.
- If what you are doing isn't working, try something else...
- When I was a kid, we didn't have smart phones. We just stared at palm-sized rocks all day...
- Back before we had iPad and smart phones, you actually had to be bored in boring meetings...
- Responding to Christ is a matter of necessity, where you attend church is a matter of taste...
- Do something really well, do it in one place and do it for a long time, and people will never forget you.
- The rougher the stretch of highway, the more clearly it identifies your true friends and supporters. Everybody cheers when you are winning.
- When friends go through tough times, it hurts...but sharing their pain is what friends are for...

- Next time I am watching a bad movie, I am going to start texting and hope some kid with a flashlight throws me out...
- A great attitude does not assure a great day, but a bad attitude assures a bad one...
- The best way to get people to listen to you is by encouraging them, not condemning them.
- You were created, gifted and empowered for a purpose. The great task of life is to live into that purpose.
- Lasting systemic change is never made quickly; it is made strategically over time.
- Realizing the role others have played in your success will always foster virtues like thanksgiving rather than vices like pride.

When, Where and Why
(Fort Worth, Texas, circa 1968)

I was saved when I was seven. Dad was holding a revival at Oak Wood Baptist Church in Ft. Worth, Texas and I walked down the aisle during the invitation; somewhere between the fortieth and forty-first verse of "Just as I Am." At that altar I repented of my dastardly deeds, prayed to receive Christ and was summarily baptized by full immersion. It is a time I remember most fondly, as I truly felt God reaching to me in some way and I responded to the best of my childhood ability. You can say what you want about childhood conversions but there is no doubt in my mind that I was saved when I was seven.

A couple years later I was just beginning my Sunday School career at the Oak Grove Baptist Church in Pinckneyville (Dad always liked Oaks). We often participated in a corporate exercise called "When, Where and Why." The idea was simple, all the elementary school aged kids got in a circle and when our turn came around we were to answer the following three questions: When did you receive Jesus? Where were you when your received Jesus? Why did you receive Jesus? The "When" responses were all recent, after all we were just kids and no one had been a Christian for very long. The "Where" responses varied but for the most part they happened at church, home or at Lake Sallateeska (a church camp south of Nashville, Illinois) where a man-made lake was dug for the expressed purpose of effecting the salvations of young Baptists. However, the "Why" was always exactly the same. Every Baptist kid I knew in the early '70's got saved because we didn't want to go to hell.

Now we had different reasons for not wanting to go to hell but let me tell you right now, *no one* wanted to go to hell.

When I was growing up, hell got a lot of work in church. In addition to sermons about hell, there were Sunday School lessons about hell, songs about hell and movies about hell. The scariest movie of them all "Burning Hell" was released in 1974 and starred a horn-rimmed Baptist preacher from Mississippi named Estus Pirkle. While it didn't win any Oscar's for cinematography, it was plenty horrifying to pre-teens from Hooterville and if you had some hell in you during the opening song, it was scared out of you by the final credits. If such means were crude evangelism tools, they were certainly effective. When I was a kid, church was the only place you ever heard the word "hell" and now church is the only place you don't hear it but I digress. My dad could preach a sermon on hell so intense that you could feel the temperature rising by the minute. There is debate as to whether the thermostat was raised mid-sermon by a secret Deacon but such accusations are unfounded (at least unproven by several Dateline investigations). By the time dad got done telling us about burning flesh, melting faces, unrelenting heat and gnawing worms, we could not wait for the invitation. We didn't walk forward, we ran forward with smoke in our eyes and singed eye brows to repent of our sins and receive Christ. Did I mention that I got saved when I was seven years old? I also got saved when I was eight, nine, nine and a half, ten, twelve and twice when I was thirteen. (Eleven was a backslidden year for me mainly spent learning to play baseball, shoot birds, cuss and smoke at Donnie Miller's house).

These days I probably don't preach on hell enough for those folks who would really like to see the fun put back into fundamentalism. I am sure Estus Pirkle would consider me only slightly ahead of Joel Osteen. Perhaps I am not sure a baptized version of "scared straight" is responsible evangelism. I do however believe in hell because the Bible believes in hell and if avoiding hell is not the best reason in the world to get saved…it sure beats not getting saved at all.

A Slice of Life

Once we had a rather eccentric neighbor pass away. Her family came in to clean up the house and invited Melissa and me inside. The house was stacked ceiling to floor with stuff and you could only get from room to room through narrow pathways. There were the contents of three houses in that house and our neighbor's treasures with which she could not bear to part were suddenly exposed after her death for what they were; junk, much of which you couldn't give away. A primary feature of Jesus' ministry was helping people see the difference between things temporal and things eternal. Being a historian and a baseball fan, I love to collect old baseball cards. One day I was admiring a Topps 1953 Satchel Paige and my daughter Lydia said, "Dad, when you die who gets stuck with your stupid baseball cards?" "Certainly not you kid…certainly not you."

Pterodactyls
(Turkey Run, Indiana, circa 2001)

Some years ago I spent the Fourth of July in Turkey Run, Indiana, at a Fellowship of Christian Athletes Camp. It was hotter than six kinds of smoke, the place looked like a prison camp, and I was spending a week teaching teenagers about Moses. It had been an incredible time of ministry. On this night I looked forward to some downtime with my daughter Lydia, the Seven Days band and the campers. As the sun set, we gathered outside greeted by Midwestern summer humidity, heat and mosquitoes the size of pterodactyls. Soon some folks came out with chilled Moon Pies and frosty bottles of Coca-Cola and when night fell the heat loosened its grip and the fireworks started. They were not great fireworks by Fourth of July standards or even good fireworks, but they were the best I will ever see because as I beheld the fireworks in the sky, I beheld the majesty of God.

Psalm 8 was a choir piece written by David. Much of the Bible cannot be understood apart from context, history, topography and culture. This passage stands on its own as perfectly on the Fourth of July today as it did in ancient Israel. As a boy shepherd David spent long nights in the Bethlehem hills protecting his father Jesse's sheep. Each evening he would get the sheep settled in a temporary fold and sleep at the entrance to keep sheep in and predators out.

On clear nights he no doubt looked into the sky and beheld a multitude of dancing stars. His mind would no doubt shift from the bleating sheep and potential dangers, to the one who created the Milky Way with the words, *"Let there be."* As David viewed God's artistry, worship flooded his being and songs of praise exploded from his spirit. Psalm 8 is one of my favorite pieces in the Bible. I'll bet the night David penned these words the sky was black as coal and stars danced like fireworks on the Fourth of July…and there were mosquitoes the size of pterodactyls!

A Candle in the Wind
(*Manchester, Georgia, circa 1991*)

Between 1989 and 1992 my family lived in Manchester, Georgia. Zec was seven and Lydia was three. Melissa and I were…younger. We had heard God's call to ministry and left our world behind to follow Jesus. I served the St. James and Chalybeate Springs United Methodist churches as pastor. These were hard times. We had no children in our congregation but our own and in three years we celebrated no births and mourned thirty deaths. We received two new members in 1990 and they quit. We had another new family come with lots of energy in 1991. They quit too. It was depressing. I served as the Youth Director for First United Methodist Church Manchester on Sunday evenings to help make ends meet. I took a full seminary load at Emory University in Atlanta for three years and navigated a three-hour round trip to get to and from school. I coached Zec's Dixie League Baseball team and played competitive softball throughout Georgia with Charlie Will Rowe and the Senoia Express.

When exhaustion settled into my bones after a couple of years, I began to wonder if it was worth it on one hand and if I was going to make it on the other. We were living off of student loans and it cost more to attend Emory each year than I made from the churches. Once a month on payday we went to Pizza Hut with the kids and ordered a large cheese pizza, a pitcher of water and played three songs on the juke box. It was as good as it got. My last year I became ill with a series of kidney stones, and as we neared the home stretch, we were running on faith, painkillers and fumes. Many nights I would not get home from school until 11:00 and I could not remember making the drive, but when I turned the final corner into the Manchester mill village that led to the parsonage at 16 Johnson Avenue, Melissa always had a burning candle in the window of our home. It reminded me that I was supported, loved and this weary season would not last forever. I couldn't wait to see that candle. Some nights I would pull into the driveway and watch that flame dance in the warm Georgia breezes and tears would come to my eyes. There was hope, God was in control and I was loved. God had a plan for my life and I was reminded of this as the tiny flame danced when there was no dancing left in me. Hope is a powerful thing and sometimes just a flicker is all you need.

- God often calls us into uncharted waters that involve steep learning curves and courageous hearts!
- Sow good things today…blessing will be in pursuit of you tomorrow!
- God cannot do anything with us until we realize it is not about us...
- One of the problems in the church today is that Christians can't hold back their cultural value judgments long enough to evangelize.
- Sometimes you have to shove on some things just to see if they will move.
- Was thinking about quitting softball to become a body builder and then I remembered softball players can still eat lots of pizza.
- Dear God, I have given everything I have today...we will try it again tomorrow. Amen.
- Jesus never bows to our expectations; He prefers to blow our minds.
- Trying to do everything ensures you will never do anything well.
- A song of praise offered to God is a song sung in defiance to the powers of this world!
- Just because people don't want the Gospel shoved down their throats, doesn't mean that people don't want the Gospel!

- We don't forgive to let those who hurt us off the hook; we forgive to break their power over us.
- Treating people well who have not treated us well is a powerful testimony to our faith...
- God's promise to us is not an absence of pain; it is a guarantee of presence.
- When you are lost...slow down. When you have clear direction...speed up!
- Many people are wrong. Few are uncertain.
- Expecting to be effective will not make you effective in and of itself, but expecting failure will ensure failure every time.
- There is no more urgent task than the development of excellent young leaders. We need them right now.
- We can't make the wind blow, but we decide every day as to whether or not to hoist a sail into the air...let's be prepared for opportunity!
- There is not a more anachronistic word than "contemporary."
- A good start does not guarantee success but it sure beats a bad start!
- There is nothing wrong with maintaining dignity in our witness. We don't have to get all obnoxious about it, but we do have to get about it.
- Never make important decisions in down cycles...
- My problem is not that I don't love some people; it is that I don't live close enough to God to let Him love them through me...

- We can never hope to be perfect Christian leaders; we can, however, be authentic ones.
- There is no form of service, discipline or sacrifice that takes the place of corporate worship in the life of a Christian.
- Treating my monster head cold by traditional means...the Lucky Charms were delicious.
- Many churches today have become Holy Ghost intolerant.
- When a church desires the presence of Christ above all else, they find they do not need anything else.
- There are people on Satan's payroll in most every congregation in USAmerica and most of them would be horrified to know who is signing their checks.
- I want "bacon's" agent. If unavailable, get me "avocado's."
- Much of what is attributed to a "lack of communication" is really a failure to plan. You can't communicate information you do not possess.

Sure, If You Blow
(San Pedro Sula, Honduras, circa 2005)

I made my first trip to San Pedro Sula, Honduras in 1985. I
went with my dad Fred Bishop and a No Greater Love
Ministries team that included Roger Lipe, Mark Jordan and
my brother-in-law Craig LeQuatte. We did a lot a street
evangelism, pioneered some sports ministry (extreme heat
edition), took an ill-advised jaunt to see the Mayan ruins in
Copan and sang Randy Stonehill songs in the city park. My
next trip was made twenty years later when a team from
Christ Church formally launched our ministry efforts in the
city. I was preaching most every night and on this stop I
was the speaker for Pastor Alejendro and his fledgling
Charismatic congregation of about 150. The sermon went
particularly well (meaning I didn't try to be funny and my
interpreter was really good) but when I tried to hand things
back to the pastor, it was clear I had not yet earned my
lempira. He had a real passion to see God move in his
people and wanted me to offer an invitation. I truly felt the
presence of the Lord in that church so after a well translated
appeal and a couple of verses from the worship team (who
compensated for a lack of musical acumen with sheer
volume) a group of about 20 lined across the front.

I knew exactly what to do! I approached the first guy and
began to pray for him with the interpreter by my side. I had
prayed for five or six folks when the pastor, tapped my
shoulder and began shaking his head in frustration, "No.

No. No." I was clearly doing something wrong. He led me back to contestant number one, placed his hand on the guy's head and began to pray in Spanish. Then he raised the volume, sort of yelled and pushed the guy backwards. Then it occurred to me, Pastor Alejendro wants these folks slain in the Spirit. I didn't think it would be helpful at this point to tell him that slaying people in the Spirit was not my primary spiritual gift. The guy who just received the "Jesus Jab" wobbled but did not go down. I must confess that I was feeling a bit better about my lack of spiritual punch but Alejendro wasn't about to give up. He got right in the guy's grill and was pointing at him and screaming at the top of his lungs. I didn't know if he was trying to get something out or get something in but it was really loud and about three quarters disturbing. He then offered another forehead chuck. The guy bobbled a bit but stayed on his feet. Frustrated beyond any words I have to describe the situation, the pastor grabbed the guy's ears and started pulling them while he yelled. I literally thought he was going to pull them off. It was like watching a spiritual boxing match, Alejendro kept hitting him harder and harder and the guy would not go down. Now a sweaty mess, Alejendro backed off momentarily, widened his stance, lowered his butt, leaned into the guy's face and blew in his face with all his might. The guy went down in a lump. Before moving to contestant number two, Alejendro put his hands on his knees, caught his breath, turned toward me, pursed his lips and with a self satisfied smirk pointed at the guy as if to say, "That is how it is done!" I looked at him and said, "Oh sure, if you blow."

I don't know if Alejendro's church start is now a mighty congregation or a distant memory but I do know this, in 2005 they had a pastor who wasn't about to quit until he saw God do something in the lives of his people.

A Slice of Life

I have a pretty good memory...on some things. I can't remember to set the trash out on Thursday evenings, but I can remember the starting lineup of the 1969 Mets or the 1964 Cardinals. I am pretty good with names but if I get the wrong one in my mind for you, I will have a difficult time replacing it with the correct one. Having a pretty good memory can also be frustrating...it should be so much better. Why can't I remember the actor's name that played Harris on Barney Miller? Why can't I remember who originally recorded "Thunder Island?" Why can't I remember who backed up Tim McCarver as catcher on the 1967 Cardinal team who defeated the Red Sox in the World Series? And why do those names suddenly come to mind, eight days after I stopped trying to remember them and I am involved in a conversation about something that actually matters? So if you are ever talking to me and I suddenly blurt out, "Dave Rickets," at least you will know what is going on.

Rev. Ralph
(Jonesboro, Illinois, circa 1966)

My first Associate Pastor at Christ Church was Rev. Ralph
Philippe. He was a retired Elder in the United Methodist
Church and was our Pastor of Visitation. Ralph was
impulsive, had a get-it-done gear like you wouldn't believe
and called it like he saw it. Ralph and I became fast friends;
we ate lunch together about five days a week and over the
eight years we shared together in ministry, he served up
many slices of his life. This was one of my favorites.

It was the summer of 1966, down in Jonesboro, Illinois, and
Ralph was appointed to the Methodist Church there to begin
his first post-seminary pastorate. That fall the church held a
revival and before the final service Ralph was informed of a
family loosely affiliated with the congregation who was in
dire financial straits. Ralph never was for hearing about a
need and not acting upon it, so that evening Ralph put out
an impassioned plea for the congregation to mobilize and
help this family. To get things started they would take an
offering. The offering was collected. The following
Sunday morning Ralph did what no Methodist pastor can
do, he offered his resignation. "People, last week I told you
about a family in this community who needed the help of
the church. We passed the plate and collected $33. I put in
$20." Now his face was purple and his voice quivered, "I
stand before you today to resign as your pastor, because I

will not serve a church that refuses to help their own."
Ralph left the sanctuary in the middle of the service, went
home and started packing.

In Ralph's long and distinguished career as a United
Methodist clergy person, there was only one short stay at a
church. The Conference Journal simply reads, "Jonesboro.
1966."

Popcorn
(Herrin, Illinois, circa 1988)

Popcorn is a wonderful thing. The best kind of popcorn is movie popcorn and I know all about making movie popcorn. In 1987 the Herrin United Methodist Church got a hold of a vision for reaching young people and built a Family Life Center. I was hired by Rev. LaVon Bayler for my inaugural church job as the Director of Family Life Ministries. The FLC had a carpeted multi-purpose gym area, an office, two meeting rooms, a weight room, a kitchen, two bathrooms, a nursery and my personal contribution, The Loft. The glass windows of the upstairs loft overlooked the basketball floor. There was linoleum flooring so people could have pizza, ice cream or birthday parties in the area. The Loft was a hang out place with a big screen television, good music and the new, deluxe popcorn popper given to us by the man who owned the movie theater. It was from Bill that I learned to make movie popcorn.

Here was the process: You flipped on a couple of heating switches and dumped the kernels into the kettle. A little coconut oil (orange, gelatinous and artery clogging) was added as an agitator moved the kernels around the heating kettle. You could hear the hum of the motor and the movement of the agitator arm as it pushed the tumbling kernels. Soon the oil would begin to sizzle ever louder and after a time you would hear a single "pop." Pop, pop, pop, pop. Soon there was a "whole lot of popping going on" and the kettle would be running over with white, fluffy popcorn and the wonderful aroma of movie popcorn would fill the entire church. I never made a fresh batch of popcorn that didn't draw a crowd of people who just "followed their nose" to the Loft. A little salt and butter made it just right.

What could be a better metaphor for the church? Every Sunday morning we bring our hard kernels to the heating kettle of worship. We add the oil of the Spirit and are stirred by the power of the Word as it agitates. We sing the songs, pray the prayers, embrace the Word and feel God's love and then it happens; someone pops. Pop! A man, who has been sitting in the pews for years, suddenly gets it! Pop! A woman who is consumed by bitterness finds the strength to forgive! Pop! A prodigal son or daughter comes home! Pop! An exploding marriage is put back together! Pop! A heart is strangely warmed! Pop! A person is called to vocational ministry! Soon there is a whole lot of popping going on. And when the church building can't contain these fired up and transformed Christians anymore, they spill out of the kettle of the church into their homes, workplaces, schools and streets. Their wonderful aroma draws the community like the smell of a fresh batch of popcorn draws customers to a concession stand. This is what the church ought to be! My prayer for the church? In the words of Orville Redenbacher, "That nearly every kernel pops!"

Plaque
(Sumner, Illinois, circa 1993)

It was late summer of 1993. Zec was 10 years old and finishing his sixth full baseball season. I had coached him for all of them. It had been a miserable year; we lost more games than we won. Many of my players were kids with marginal talent at best and many of the parents were less than objective on the relative skill of the offspring. (Do I still sound a little bitter?) I counted the days until the season ended. Finally the big day came, the end of the season awards. I knew the ritual. I give the kids their trophies, say a few nice things about each player (hoping my nose didn't noticeably grow) and then someone interrupts me, tells me what a great coach I am and gives me a plaque.

I liked those plaques; my office was full of them. On tough days I would look at all my trophies, certificates and plaques to remind me that I am not really such a bad guy. The ceremony began and I did my part, but no one interrupted me despite the many chances I gave them to do so. There was no applause, no thank you and certainly no plaque. Stunned, I concluded and everyone quickly went home. Each kid left carrying a trophy (didn't you used to have to accomplish something to win a trophy?) but the coach got nothing, zippo, nada, the big skunk-aroo-no, the only plaque I had was on my teeth.

I was alone in the universe. At first I reflected on how sorry the kids were. I doubted any of them would ever find work. Then it occurred to me they were destined to be sorry with that group of parents; ingrates that they were. They obviously had no idea of how blessed they were to have me for a coach. I was feeling underappreciated, ignored, taken advantage of and just a little depressed. Then the voice of the Lord spoke to me (or something did). Did I spend my whole summer coaching for a $10 plaque made of laminated pressboard to appease my ego? If I did, I was an unabashed idiot. Was I so petty that I needed the half-hearted accolades of a handful of people who cared little about me to justify my efforts? What is driving this thing? That day I realized I was a sick man. That was the last year *that* Shane Bishop ever coached. The Shane Bishop who coached the following year did it to teach a great game, make a difference in the lives of young people, spend time with his son, influence parents for Jesus Christ and to show God's love to my community. It was the best year I ever had! We won game after game, several baseball families came into the church and it was fun. The difference? I was coaching for the right reasons and it made all the difference in the world. They even gave me a plaque.

- When being polite becomes a greater core value than telling the truth, we run into authenticity problems.
- I figure we are all crazy...I just want to be God's kind of crazy.
- The "sin that so easily besets you" needs to be drowned in baptismal water every day.
- Every sinful and hurtful thing begins with a single impulse not brought under the submission of Christ.
- Playing in the water with my grandsons got rained out today...
- An e-mail I just read ended with these words, "Save the earth, it's the only planet with chocolate."
- A lack of contentment will steal the happiness from your life on one hand and entice you toward terminal stupidity on the other.
- We can't change our yesterdays, but we can receive Holy Spirit power to live a new tomorrow.
- The Sadducees did not mind God moving; they just needed Him to move in ways that didn't affect their theology, bank accounts or politics.
- When we are living the Spirit-filled life, God will sometimes lead us into situations out of which only God can deliver us!
- US America needs a new template for manhood. The old one has failed.

- I can personally guarantee that 100% of the invitations to Christ we fail to offer will result in nothing.
- The Biblical idea of "lost" is much closer to "temporarily misplaced" than "eternally doomed." Jesus came to seek and save the lost.
- Financial generosity for the Christian is not an act of depletion; it is an act of renewal.
- The first question I ask prospective Christian leaders is, "Are you called?" The second is, "Do you have the stomach for this?"
- I am often tempted to add Spanish as a "Language I know" to my profile but then reality hits me...I speak Spanish like Tarzan spoke English.
- Being on vacation while staying home is like retirement practice.
- There is an entertainment element to good preaching, but if substance and insight are sacrificed, the price got too high.
- A godly impulse that we do not act upon is a wasted impulse.
- What a tragedy so many Christians only use the name of Jesus to politely wrap up a prayer. The name of Jesus is polite like dynamite.
- Many people put in a fraction of the time required for success and legitimately wonder why their ventures so often fail.
- We are all going to error, why not error on the side of grace?

- Jesus always preferred a wolf dressed like a wolf to a wolf dressed like a sheep.
- Hear Jesus say to you as he did Zacchaeus, "I must come to your house today."
- Memorial Day is a wonderful opportunity to recognize how much of the wonderful life we enjoy was made possible by the sacrifice of others.
- We all come to Jesus for our own reasons. There is just one reason He comes to us...love.
- After playing four softball games and now sitting, something is happening to my body that is not supposed to happen until after you die.
- Here is something no preacher has ever said, "How will we handle the overflow crowds on Memorial Day weekend?"
- In a softball game with possible theological implications, Christ Church/Worth defeated the Devil Dogs in a short game victory...
- The big idea of Christianity is never to try harder; it is an invitation to be transformed entirely.
- I saw a bumper sticker that read, "Visualize Whirled Peas." Consider it done.

I've Got That Going for Me
(Marion Federal Penitentiary Work Camp, circa 1985)

I served as the Director of Family Life Ministries at First United Methodist Church in Herrin, Illinois from 1986-1989. While there we played a few softball games against the Work Camp team at the Federal Penitentiary in Marion. Baseball legend Pete Rose was there for a short while but he never played on the softball team. (This was a disappointment to me but has nothing to do with this story.) It was an interesting experience for our church league team to go through the stringent processes required to pull off such an evangelism endeavor. I still remember being searched for weapons, our equipment being X-rayed for drugs and being treated like a potential criminal. (Today we call this routine security for a domestic plane flight). It was truly a bit unnerving when the gate closed behind us and we were on the "inside." On this particular Saturday afternoon we played a double header. I remember that we split the two games, they were better offensively than defensively and the umpiring fell something short of "fair and impartial." I also remember that I had a terrific afternoon both at the plate and in the field. When we had finished saying a prayer, shaking hands with the opposition and were headed for the van, the prison team coach put his arm around my neck as we walked, "Man, if you ever fall on hard times, I want you to know you have a spot on this team anytime." "Well," I thought, "I've got that going for me!"

A Slice of Life

I will often ask Melissa if she wants a backrub and she will almost always decline. It is not that she doesn't want a back rub; it is that she hates to give them and receiving one would make her feel bad. It is like when a distant relative sends you a Christmas gift. You don't rejoice in the gift; you grumble the gesture will have to be returned. The reason we struggle with forgiveness is because of that pesky part in the Lord's Prayer, "*Forgive us our trespasses as we forgive those who have trespassed against us*." The gift of the cross is hard to accept because if we receive the forgiveness it offers, we must offer that same forgiveness to others. A lot of people would rather pass.

Dolly
(Sumner, Illinois, circa 1994)

I never will forget the Sunday morning Dolly walked into the Sumner church in the summer of 1994. She was somewhere between twenty-five and fifty and wore stained clothing five sizes too small for her rotund body. Her fingernails were filthy, her hair was filthy and her feet were filthy. Dolly's acrid scent permeated the sanctuary. I would literally hold my breath to keep from gagging when I was within five feet of her. Behind her trailed three ragamuffin urchins resembling their mother in every way. Rodney was 10, Bill was 8 and Erica was 6. I sensed from the very beginning that God was keeping a careful eye on how we treated Dolly. We were a growing, dynamic church containing the franchised, educated and powerful of the tiny community. Dolly would be a test for us all.

Soon, Dolly, Rodney, Bill and Erica were regular fixtures. The complaints poured into my office. Wherever Dolly chose to sit, the odor was so intense that people sitting around her became physically ill. Her two boys were whirling cyclones prone to violence and shaped by a lifetime of neglect and abuse. When they would act up in church, Dolly would literally grab them by the ears and drag them out. She would seldom get to the back door before she would begin profanely swearing at the top of her lungs. A lot of good Methodists learned new words every

Sunday. We tried to help. We sent a work team to clean her house. The horrified team reported gaping holes in the flooring, no running water, animal feces, mountains of dishes and swarms of roaches eating various molding snack foods laying all over the disheveled house. We paid her water bill and brought in a used washing machine and hooked it up. We gave the family new clothes. Still, each week Dolly brought the children to church in filthy clothes, food caked to their faces and reeking of body odor. I don't ever recall seeing any of them in the clothes we gave them.

Neither church nor state could get Dolly to help herself or to improve the environment in which she was raising her children. And all the while I felt God's piercing eyes upon us and heard Him saying that Dolly was His child and we had better treat her right. One day an unofficial spokesman came into my office and informed me that several of our families could bear it no longer. They were going to leave the church. They were truly sorry, exasperated, out of ideas and could take no more of Dolly. These were good families. They gave their offerings each week, came every Sunday morning and evening and helped where needed. Their absence would be devastating to the congregation. There was not one point brought before me with which I disagreed. Dolly smelled, she shouldn't have those children, she was abusive, her home was a pigsty, her kids were disruptive and the church was in chaos the moment they stepped in the door. She and those kids would never contribute a dime, had cost us a fortune and were driving off the very people who tried to help her. Yet there was Dolly, created from the dust in the image of God, with all that dust and more still on her. Something inside her troubled mind told her that her family needed to be in church and they attended each Sunday oblivious of the tsunami they were causing. I told the spokesman to tell his people to do what they had to do, but Dolly and her children would be welcomed as long as I was the pastor. But before they quit the church in mass, I asked them to read James 2:1-13 and let me know what they thought.

When people read James' thoughts on the poor and that there will be no mercy for us if we are unmerciful to others, they were cut to the heart; no one quit the church and Dolly was welcomed each week. Within a year and a half, both bill collectors and the Department of Children and Family Services were growing impatient; she had burned most of the bridges people of good will had extended to her. One day, she took her children, loaded them into a car that barely ran and left town. She left bills unpaid, the shack to the roaches and dogs, the filthy clothes where they lay; the clean clothes we gave her folded in a pile and didn't look back. She didn't need a moving van. The television fit in the trunk and little else was worth taking. She was gone as quickly as she had come; I must confess there was a sense of relief for me. It was the kind of relief you feel when you turn in a final exam over material you barely understood and though you didn't ace it, you passed. We had done well, for in welcoming Dolly, we had welcomed Christ.

A Story About Friendship (Bread)
(Atlanta, Georgia, circa 1993)

I remember my first bite! The chocolate bread was still hot and there was a sugar glaze on the top. It was amazing...did I mention it was amazing? Amish Friendship Bread is truly a unique experience. It is not a food; it is a life form. It takes ten full days to start a batch, once it is started; it multiplies at a rate unthinkable in the non-rabbit world as long as you feed it with a pinch of sugar every couple of days. The idea is that you make a batch, put it into three containers, give two away to friends and keep one for yourself. It is truly a lovely idea. The problem is that after a while you run out of friends and the batter keeps growing like compound interest on a college student's credit card.

One year it was vacation time and we had no less than nine starts of Amish Friendship Bread. Not knowing what to do, Melissa took the nine Tupperware containers with us. We were in the dog days of August and we pointed our Oldsmobile station wagon south toward Atlanta. One afternoon after a several hour excursion, we returned to the 120-degree interior of our vehicle to witness something truly awful. The heat had apparently exacerbated the multiplication process and the nine starts had built up gas, blown the Tupperware lids off the containers and all the batter had supernaturally oozed into every crevice the car featured. The odor of dying yeasty dough was overwhelming and the clean-up job was simply impossible. We rode for months in our yeasty car of death with the windows down. I have never had a single craving for a piece of Amish Friendship Bread since that time.

When you stop feeding Amish Friendship Bread, it dies. When you keep feeding it, it grows. Let's feed the things that bring life and starve the things that have no place in our lives...or in our Oldsmobiles.

Could You Possibly Stop With the Sayings of Rev. Shane?

- It is mathematically impossible to make a comeback when you haven't been anywhere...
- I now own a 1948 Bowman Stan Musial rookie card! I would like to thank all the people whose weddings I performed last year for making it possible.
- When it comes to effecting change in the church, I will take one "on fire" Christian over a hundred programs.
- Sometimes Jesus loves on me and sometimes Jesus shoves on me. What He never does is conform to what I think He ought to be.
- Heard the world was going to end Saturday. I will be in Iowa. Never thought I would be in Iowa when the world ended...
- The thing about hoarders is the more they get, the less they have.
- I love to come to church each Sunday. No matter how bad our week, we get to look into the tomb and see that He is not there...
- Pastors should be excited on Sundays like NFL coaches are excited on Sundays. And equally prepared...
- Experiencing discontinuity does not mean you are doing something wrong; it means you are doing something!

- Visionaries dream alone. Leaders take people with them.
- Jesus is always asking of us what we least want to give Him.
- Worry is a conviction that God can't do His job unless you have an ulcer.
- I have my doubts but I am becoming suspicious of them.
- "To dwell on worry is to invite a thief into your life and just tell him to take what he wants!"
- The best thing a person can do for their family is to put God first in their life!
- A lot of people are hoping the Mocha frappe machine at church is in good working order tomorrow morning...or perhaps it is just me.
- There is nothing more powerful than having someone in your life who believes in you!
- Cinco de Mayo proves that US Americans love to celebrate so much that we are willing to invent a holiday for another country.
- Want to truly influence people? Begin by truly caring about them...
- Tragedy has a way of reminding us how little of what we stress and obsess upon really matters.
- The Road to Emmaus story reminds us the lost are not always thieves on crosses; they are sometimes disciples walking the wrong direction.
- How often do we lose sight of a larger hope in the face of a small disappointment?

- Listening is the price we pay for the opportunity to speak in this new world; it is really a better deal for everyone involved.
- Peter's response to the news of the women at the tomb reminds us of why a shot at redemption is always worth a morning run...
- Effective Christian evangelists can't hide in the Christian sub-culture. There just aren't enough good prospects there...
- The resurrection of Christ is what most separates Christianity from other religions. It is our boldest claim and most defining.
- The key to preaching an Easter sermon is resisting the temptation to try to be brilliant.
- Those who dare to make a leap of faith find their feet land on the most real thing in the cosmos, resurrection of Jesus Christ!
- I played high school football back in the days when they thought dehydration built character in young men...
- The problem with blaming others is that it's never quite clear who is supposed to fix the problem. Take responsibility. Fix it.

A Radically Egalitarian Place
(Belleville, Illinois, circa 1999)

Last week I made a pastoral call to Memorial Hospital.
There is something radically egalitarian about a hospital.
You would never realize this from the parking lot. There
you see sleek, new, techno packed and leather trimmed
Lexus automobiles sitting next to dinged and rusted 1983
Gremlins with ripped cloth seats and the hood wired on.
The people getting out of their automobiles usually match
their cars quite well. You don't have to be a sociologist to
see that the people walking into the hospital come from
different worlds. But when you go into the hospital waiting
room, some similarities begin to occur. People in the
waiting room are tense, have uptight and worried faces and
each time a door opens, they look to see if the doctor is
bringing them news. When they realize the messenger did
not come for them, their attentions quickly return to their
magazine, their conversation or the television set. People in
waiting rooms are isolated, helpless and exhausted. I see
people conversing in waiting rooms who would never speak
to each other in the parking lot.

Distinctions fade even more when you move further inside.
The patients on the floors seem remarkably uniform. They
don't have on street clothes, jewelry, make-up or toupees
and their partials are out. They are all miserable, restless,
drugged up, having bad hair days and have bruises on their

arms. The one size fits all blue paper gowns simultaneously rob them of individuality, modesty and fashion sense. But the playing field is not truly leveled until you enter the Intensive Care Unit area. There, all distinctions melt away. People are harnessed to machines that monitor them, medicate them, feed them, hydrate them, rid them of fluids and breathe for them. In an ICU, life and death are fighting it out, everyone looks alike and nothing outside that room matters. The neighborhood in which they reside, the size of their investment portfolio, *who they are*, *who they know* or the make of car they have in the lot is suddenly the least important thing in the world. There they lay with two eyes, two hands, one mouth, one brain and one soul with a void only God can fill. Desperate people look a whole lot the same. They look like us.

A Slice of Life

While Melissa and I were in the Smoky Mountains a few years ago, we visited the Methodist Church in Cades Cove and stumbled upon a real life Smoky Mountain wedding! The preacher invited us to have a seat; from the opening to the final broom hop, we sat through all ten minutes of the ceremony. We talked a lot about weddings after that wonderful experience. Our discussion reiterated that there are a lot of differences between girls and guys. It is in far less than one percent of the weddings that I have officiated that the groom has asked for any meaningful participation in the planning of the wedding. The reason is clear; the wedding has been planned in the mind of the bride since she was nine years old and the groom is nearly extraneous. To quote Melissa, "All little girls have their weddings planned to the smallest detail. The only variable, and a minor one at that, is 'insert guy here.'" I am glad she inserted me some thirty years ago.

A Baseball Story (I Like Baseball)
(Anywhere, USA circa timeless AD)

I am a St. Louis Cardinal fan. It is not mandatory that I do not like the Yankees (as juxtaposed with our signed covenant to hate the Cubs), but I somewhat resent the Yankees. They have an infinite amount of money to spend in the building of their team and the Cardinals have to do it on a budget. It is like a guy who works in a factory being expected to own a home in the same neighborhood as the CEO of a Fortune 500 company. The Cardinals defeated the Yankees in the 1964 World Series (Thanks Bob Gibson) and I hope they never have to play them again. Sometimes you should quit while you are ahead. The only thing I like about the New York Yankees is that they don't put the players name on the back of the uniform. If Babe Ruth, Lou Gerhrig, Yogi Berra, Mickey Mantle and Joe DiMaggio didn't get their name on their backs, these modern players don't either. If just being a part of the most successful baseball franchise in history and wearing the pinstripes isn't enough for you...that is just too bad. I like that. If I owned a pro sports team, the first thing I would do is rip the names off the backs of the uniforms.

It is of interest to me that our Christ Church softball teams do not put the name of the players on the back of our uniforms. We put the name of our savior on the front! There is surely some responsibility that comes from wearing His uniform. When we asked Jesus Christ to come into our lives as Savior and Lord, we became part of the most dynamic team in history; the Church of Jesus Christ. The church was founded at Pentecost and is empowered by the Holy Spirit to be the most powerful force on the planet. If I played for the Cardinals, I would be jazzed to put on the same uniform worn by the Gashouse Gang, Stan Musial, Ken Boyer, Lou Brock and Albert Pujols. It would be enough to wear the "birds on the bat" across my chest…I wouldn't need my name on the back. Christ Church, do you realize we put on the same uniform worn by Abraham, Moses, John the Baptist, Paul, Augustine, John Calvin, John Wesley, Mother Teresa and Billy Graham? If they didn't get their names on their backs, it isn't looking good for us either. It is enough just to wear the uniform.

Another Baseball Story (I Really Like Baseball)
(Anywhere, USA circa timeless AD)

I have watched a lot of St. Louis Cardinal baseball for a lot of years now and I have made an observation; Cardinal fans like players with dirty uniforms and they *love* players with blood on their uniforms. I really liked to watch Pete Rose play when I was a kid. Sure he could hit but boy could he play! He was always the dirtiest and bloodiest guy on the team. Pete's sole mission was to win and he played all out every time he stepped on to the field. The church has a single mission; *to connect people with Jesus Christ.* Our pursuit of this mission makes us participants in a glorious adventure in which we work toward the salvation of the world. The Bible talks about "So great a cloud of witnesses" who watch the Church as we play this earthly game. I wonder if they like the way we play the game? Do we give them something about which to cheer?

In the church of Jesus Christ, each of us are expected to do what God instructs us to do, what opportunity allows us to do and what the Spirit equips us to do. In short, we are called to play hard. The success of the Christian is not measured by touchdowns, points, goals or runs but by effective service and absolute obedience. I will do what He asks me to do, I will give what He asks me to give, go where He calls me to go and serve where He asks me to serve. I don't want the game of life to end and my uniform to be clean. I don't want to hear booing from the stands when they call my name. Let's face it church, if there wasn't a little blood on our uniforms, there would be no team at all.

- War after war, disaster after disaster, heartbreak after heartbreak, faith is hope that will not be quieted.
- Religion as a general concept is a great way to control people but a poor way to empower them. Relationship is another thing entirely.
- It is precisely because we can trust our lives to God that we can trust our deaths to God.
- An open door is an opportunity. A closed door is a revelation.
- I spent many years skeptical of the relationship between faith and emotion. I am now convinced that to believe is to feel.
- We want to rush to Easter but it comes slowly...in God's own time.
- We cannot earn the right to eat and drink at Christ's table. It is a gift to be received.
- God will never reveal Himself to us in ways that negate the need for faith!
- Isn't it amazing how all those things in our lives we "just wish would go away," somehow keep us close to God?
- "Lead us not into temptation" is a prayer best prayed with the assistance of clear boundaries.
- Luke's Palm Sunday story is ironically, palm less.

- The part I love best about writing sermons is when your fingers get to preaching as you pound the keyboard.
- I think the hole in most of our lives is the gap between good intention and meaningful action.
- The rich, young ruler was asked to sever his tie with that which he loved more than God. The same is asked of us.
- Materialism is a religion of accumulation and all it can promise is more of what it has failed to deliver in the first place.
- I have no patience these days for critics who do nothing, have opinions about everything and feel the need to speak.
- Leadership is everything. Whatever the question is, leadership is the answer.
- I have given up cynicism. It is just too easy...
- Jesus always treated common sinners way too well for the church folk to tolerate...
- The need to be seen as brilliant is a defense mechanism...
- If you want to lead people, you are going to have to be someone to whom people can relate.
- If God made you, God loves you. Period. End of story.
- Pastors need to stop expecting committees to do what God has called them to do.

- When God wants something done, God calls a leader. This is a very different thing than forming a committee...
- It is interesting to me that no one would start a church these days and name it "First."
- The ultimate goal of Christianity is not to be first but to be in relationship with God and dwell in His house forever!
- When I think of the prodigal story, I see a father desperately trying to keep his family together. People can relate to that.
- Choose well the people with whom you choose to associate; they will define your life.
- A lot of people don't care about the other parts of the Bible; they just want to read the parts that Jesus wrote.
- Doing ministry in a fallen world is hard work but if the leaders do not have the courage to enforce church discipline, it is impossible work.
- You can't always run at 200 MPH. You have to slow down for the turns.

The Power of Prayer (In the Frozen Food Aisle)
(Sumner, Illinois, circa 1994)

In my five years as pastor of the Sumner/Beulah Charge, I seldom had time to visit our shut-ins with any regularity. Sumner ran about 225 a Sunday and Beulah ran about 110; either congregation should have been a full time job. When you factored in that the nearest real hospital was an hour and a half away, there was seldom time to do anything but sermon preparation, attend church meetings and visit the sick. It really wasn't as bad as you might think on the shut-in front because I often ran into them at Wal-Mart, the restaurant at Red Hill State Park or the Key Market Grocery Store. One day I was picking something up for Melissa at the Key Market and saw one of our Sumner shut-ins in the canned goods aisle. She had spotted me first and was hoping to avoid me by looping around the frozen food section and making a getaway while I was in the back of the store. This was unbelievably ambitious for an 88 year old woman with limited mobility in a 1,800 square foot grocery store but she gave it a try. Sensing her dubious intentions, I sprinted back to the front of the store, looped around and when she arrived at the frozen foods aisle, I was standing face to face with her. I smiled and asked, "How are you doing today?" She was now in an old fashioned conundrum. She has stated on many occasions that she was too ill to attend church but here she was standing under her own power (and moving with surprising speed) at the Key Market. I couldn't wait for her response. She looked down, gathered her wits, took a long breath and started outlining her maladies for me from the top of her psoriasis afflicted scalp to the bottom of her hammer toes.

When she had talked herself out, I said, "Sister, can I pray for you?" She responded, "Right here in the frozen food aisle?" I said, "Yes mam" and jumped right in. I did not use the "inside voice" mom had taught me as a kid and launched into a ten minute, high volume prayer in which I asked God to heal each of her various illnesses and discomforts by name. I prayed that her mysterious "Sunday Sickness" that prohibited her from worshipping with God's people but allowed her to shop in grocery stores would be healed and hit on various and sundry other petitions for her as I felt led. When I finished, she thanked me and was moving toward the door so quickly that she almost forgot to pay.

If you are wondering about the after-effects of our holy encounter, I am pleased to report that a miracle occurred! I ran into the same shut-in a few weeks later at the Wal-Mart in Lawrenceville, caught her eye and yelled across the store, "Great to see you, how are you feeling today?" She replied a resounding, "FANTASTIC!" The Lord works in mysterious ways.

A Slice of Life

When I travel, I spend a certain amount of time lost. Lost is probably a bit inaccurate, because I always know where I am but am often uncertain about the relationship of where I am to my desired destination. Before I go on a road trip, I always chart my path but somewhere along the way I am very likely to miss a turn, get funneled onto the wrong road or run into something causing a detour. Sometimes I am so wrapped up in singing along with George Straight or Rich Mullins that by the time I reestablish my connection with time and space, I am a hundred miles off the path. To be honest, I really don't mind being lost because I get to see things folks never see who follow directions. I often find out of the way restaurants (some good and some terrible), incredible Victorian houses, interesting historical sites and architecturally interesting town squares. Many is the time that I have been blissfully lost, taking in new sights and sounds, while my passengers in the car are stressed out of their minds. There is a lot I do when I travel that may possibly be annoying to passengers but I do understand one concept: life doesn't happen where you planned to be, are supposed to be or where you hoped you would be; life happens where you are.

A Football Story (It's Really About Dad and Me)
(*San Antonio, Texas, circa 1974*)

As a boy, there were three holy services of worship each Sunday. There was Sunday morning church, Sunday evening church and Sunday afternoon football. Dad officiated at all three. When the Dallas Cowboys played, all else stopped for three hours and the future of all humanity hung precariously in the outcome. As is his way, when he enters earth, he enters like a whirlwind! He would hang on every play. Hoot, holler, clap and groan. If the Cowboys lost a close one, he struggled to preach that night. *How can a man proclaim hope in the midst of such agony?*

Football holds some of my fondest memories of my childhood. Some of my best times with my dad were spent in front of a black and white, rabbit eared, twelve-inch television. I remember *Family Night* each Monday in the fall and winter. Don't be misled by the name, dad and I would watch football; mom and Jill went somewhere else. It was Fred and Shane night and it was the best night of the week. The evening was spent with *Gunsmoke* and *Monday Night Football*. Matt Dillon and Tom Landry, how could it get better than that! For this event mom made peanut-butter-chocolate-oatmeal no-bake cookies. I would prepare by garnering all of my football cards of the respective teams playing that evening. I would choose the team I was rooting for and dad got the other one. We watched the game with the cards lined horizontally in front of us. Each time Howard Cosell, Frank Gifford or Dandy Don Meredith mentioned a name represented by a football card, you moved the card ahead a full length. Like a horserace the game sprawled in front of us, as quarterbacks and running backs pulled from the pack. Names of football players became a part of my life and vocabulary. I knew every player on the Dallas Cowboys and I dreamed that I was Roger Staubach, Tony Dorsett or Bob Lilly at night. My eyes got heavy somewhere after halftime; when I awakened the cards were cleaned up, the TV was off and I was in bed. My dad! There was a man who knew how to party!

Football was an earthly vice that forced dad into the world of normalcy. It was a transition back into our world and we appreciated his presence, if just for a while. Football has remained a realm uninterrupted by pastoral emergencies, the underground church in communist lands, No Greater Love, Mardi Gras or next Sunday's sermon. Football was a plane on which my dad and I could sit side by side…in two seats, right on the fifty yard line!

Bawling Calves
(Great Smoky Mountain National Park, Tennessee, circa 1978)

In 1978, dad and I went on a two-man vacation to the Great Smoky Mountains. We had been many times before but this week it was just the two of us. He was at the age where a man looks younger than he is and I was at the age where a teenager looks older than he is. *Everyone* thought we were brothers. I say everyone because we did not encounter one person for seven straight days to which dad did not speak. Dad's Plan A strategy of initiating conversation involves hypothesizing upon an initial point of reference and commenting on it in a familiar way. His immediate goal is to transform himself from a *"them* to an *us"* as quickly as possible in the mind of his soon-to-be-made best friend. If a guy has on a Cubs hat, dad will talk to him about the Chicago Cubs as if he has been a Cubs fan for his entire life. He can do the same with any professional baseball, basketball, hockey or football team. He can also do the same with any city in the world but he is best with Christians. If he finds a family is of the Southern Baptist persuasion, dad will open the Baptist file in his brain and in four minutes you would think he had known these people for his entire life. He can also do the same with Methodist, Presbyterians, Charismatics and Catholics. (I will tell you about nuns in Czechoslovakia another time.)

When there is not a clear tip as to a conversational *in*, dad resorts to Plan B. He uses humor. Well, it is something akin to humor. As a boy it always amazed me that dad watched Hee Haw. I never recall him listening to country and western music at any other time. It's not just country music; dad just isn't a music guy at all. He only knows one song and it is U2's "I Still Haven't Found What I'm Looking For" which he still calls "These City Walls" after twenty-five years. (To my knowledge, neither Buck Owens nor Roy Clark ever covered it on Hee Haw.) As I look back, the mystery of his love for Hee Haw has been solved. He wasn't watching to be entertained; he was gathering ammunition for his big magnum extrovert gun! He watched Hee Haw the way a scout watches a baseball game, an aspiring preacher listens to a great sermon or a surgeon watches an experimental operation.

While we were descending the Chimneys Tops in the Great Smokies, we passed a gaggle of women who were on their way up the steep and rocky path. I flinched waiting to see what dad would say to *this* group of total strangers as they passed. When they were within earshot, too loudly and with far too much enthusiasm, dad exclaimed, "Ladies, I feel like a farmer. My calves are bawling." I still consider this a low point in my life. Like no other time before or since, I wished I had never been born and that dad had never owned a television.

A Slice of Life

My dad reports that some years ago on an evangelism trip to the New Orleans Mardi Gras the Spirit of God descended upon a street church. There were 300 guys playing instruments and singing in the French Quarter and God showed up! The praise got so lively that the Baptists started shouting, the Pentecostals began to speak in tongues, the Presbyterians lifted their hands and the Charismatics started dancing. It was also reported that one of the Methodists got so excited that he took one of his hands out of his pocket.

Stuckey's
(A Stuckey's in Oklahoma, circa 1970)

When I was about eight, we were traveling cross country and stopped at a Stuckey's for some gas. Stuckey's were wonderful places with food, gas, shot glasses with the names of states on them and such high tech video offerings as "Pong" unfolding in green and black. I guess a Cracker Barrel store is about the closest we come today but retro/folksy can't even begin to compare to the sheer, shamelessly commercialized wonder of Stuckey's. I was looking around the store and found a little pocket knife. It was a beauty; low quality blade forged of cheap metals, plastic casing and the name of a state printed on it. It was where form met function and function became art for a second grader.

With wide eyes and a thirst for adventure, I asked dad if I could have it. Like an episode of "Kung Fu," dad flashed back to his life when he was eight. By that time he was driving tractors, butchering hogs and hunting wild game with a shotgun. Uncharacteristically confused by nostalgia and blinded to the realization he was raising a late bloomer, dad bought the knife for me. I walked back to the car feeling the euphoria that comes only to an armed man. It felt good to be packing heat and I found myself hoping for some type of disturbance calling for the swift and decisive action of an armed child missing both of his front teeth.

When we climbed into the car, I proudly showed mom, who said, "*Fred, he is too young to have a pocketknife.*" I smiled and defiantly took the knife out of my pocket, pried it open and ran the blade completely through my thumb. One of us got in a lot of trouble. The other got a Band-Aid.

More Sayings of Rev. Shane

- Ironically, the more I understand grace, the better I become...
- Spent the night replacing my basement sump pump...life in the fast lane, my friends.
- Without evangelism, the church becomes an organism without a reproductive system.
- Christian growth more often occurs as we struggle with difficult things, than when we have our familiar positions affirmed.
- Most of us were formally educated to succeed in a world that no longer exists.
- Living in a region with a lot of really excellent churches makes all of our churches better!
- The problem with really legalistic, uptight and judgmental people is that they can't even live up to their own standards.
- Seminary prepared me for a piano, organ and church bulletin world. I graduated with honors perfectly prepared to do ministry in 1958...
- I used to wear a hat a lot for a guy who still had all his hair. Now I am just a guy who wears a hat a lot...
- Alter your church space to fit your ministry. Don't design your ministry to fit your space. Moving walls is cheap and easy.
- God's strength comes as we need it..."give us this day our daily bread."

- Feed a cold. Feed a fever.
- God can handle our doubts, our anger and our utter helplessness in times of tragedy. That is one of the things I love best about God!
- Some days are filled with joy and some days are filled with pain. God is God of all days...
- The whole message of the Gospel is that we get better than we deserve.
- It is of interest to me that none of the three parables about lost and found things in Luke 15 are interested in casting blame...
- The presence of money in a life will only exacerbate an absence of character.
- The chief complaint of the holy rollers against Jesus was that He socialized with turncoats and drunks.
- Never confuse how humans misuse freewill for God's will...
- Leadership is a simple concept. Now moving beyond the conceptual stage is another matter entirely.
- People do what they want to do...not what you want for them to do. Control is an illusion.
- Leadership that is not strategic is not leadership.
- Once you know a person's character and core values, their actions get highly predictable...
- Answer the big questions and the small ones get easy...
- Christian leadership is the simplest thing in the world...in theory.

- Too many churches are going nowhere; why would anyone want to go there with them?
- I just got an ad on Facebook for cans of Holy Land Sand. I don't know about you but I am feeling closer to Jesus already.
- Leaders are creators of culture. As to whether this is a blessing or a curse says a lot about the leader.
- My mission of "connecting people to Jesus Christ" has never changed; my strategies for accomplishing that mission are in constant negotiation.
- Nothing wears me out like doing nothing.
- Truth delivered without humility is still truth...it just doesn't taste very good.
- Only God can make the Spirit winds to blow but good leaders keep a sail close by...

Bribes of the Son
(DuQuoin, Illinois, circa 1978)

When I was in high school grade card days could be tense. They were days calling for strategy, cunning and yes, even bribery. One semester I received the letter grade of D+ in Sophomore Algebra. My first thought was, "Perhaps this was a mistake." When I asked my teacher how I possibly could have received a D+, he said it was because he gave me credit on problems up to the point I missed them. To verify, he pulled out my latest exam. It was a gruesome thing covered with red ink. It truly pained me to see it again. Upon my quick examination, it appeared that I managed to provide the incorrect answer on every single equation. Had he not extended me that courtesy, I would never have passed his class. It seemed senseless to continue our conversation so I thanked him and moved on to Plan B.

With fear and trepidation I pondered how to properly take this utterly unacceptable grade card (representing nine weeks of academic neglect) to my father. Then it came to me; like a lightning bolt from heaven, an epiphany came to me! On the way home I stopped by Allen's Neighborhood Grocery and purchased dad an ice cold Coca-Cola (pulled from a real ice chest in a glass bottle) and a frozen Snickers Bar (his favorite), hoping that since morning he had grown addle-minded and was suddenly susceptible to cheap bribes. When I arrived at home via the back alley from Allen's, I found him sitting in the back yard. I excitedly presented him with my thoughtful gifts (bribes) and he said, "Let's see it." He took a quick look, handed back the card and said without energy, "You are grounded for a month." With that he leaned back in his lawn chair, took a cleansing breath, smiled at his good fortune and consumed the bribes of the son, savoring every drop and morsel.

A Slice of Life

When I was a freshman at DuQuoin High School, I had a
P.E. class with the seniors. There must have been three or
four of us freshman in the class. We never knew how we
came to be in that class but we ruled out good luck right
away. One day they were picking up sides for a basketball
game. The field was quickly narrowing between seniors
with no athletic acumen whatsoever and freshmen. One of
the seniors said to the captain, "Pick Bishop." The captain
looked at my six foot one, 142-pound sliver of
uncoordination, scowled and responded curtly, "*We don't
want him.*" I would say it didn't affect me but I still
remember it. I was raised in a tradition that celebrated *me*
picking Jesus. Though that is necessary, I don't think that
is the front page headline: The front page reads ***Jesus
Picked Me***!

The Adams' Family
(*San Antonio, Texas, circa 1973*)

It was the fall of 1973. The year before dad had left the pastoral ministry and moved our family to San Antonio, Texas. He became part of an evangelistic ministry founded by evangelist Sammy Tippit called ***God's Love in Action***. They did street ministry and smuggled Bibles into communist countries. To say the job didn't pay well would be misleading; it didn't pay at all. We lived by faith and times were lean. Novembers are hard to spot in San Antonio. The desert Mesquite trees don't produce beautiful foliage. In fact, I only remember two seasons: eleven months of summer and one month of rain.

It was Thanksgiving Eve and I remember mom had been crying all day. After Wednesday church, mom grimly announced the Thanksgiving menu with tears in her eyes. We were having Spam, potatoes, green beans and perhaps a glass of tea for everyone. No turkey, no dressing, no pumpkin pie. We awakened slightly less than thankful; my thoughts could not help but drift back to Illinois where our cousins would be gathering in Sunfield for a feast. Somehow the scent of Spam heating in the oven does not fill my heart with sentimentality.

The phone rang. It was the Adams family from church. I don't remember much about them except they had a girl

125

about my age named Noel. They said they had more food than they could possibly eat and wondered if we might be free to share Thanksgiving with them. Would we? Shouts of joy echoed throughout our home. God had not forgotten us! Mom put the cans of Spam, green beans and the jar of tea back in the nearly bare cupboard. The potatoes we would eat another day. I saw that a spontaneous act of love by one family could change the orbit of another. I saw the church at its best that day. Not organized, programmed and slick but genuine, authentic and love infested. One family acted upon their impulse and grace fell upon another.

Something wonderful happened that day between the Adams and Bishop families. We were two families who needed each other! They had too many empty chairs around a bulging table and we had too little food. Love is a powerful thing. It is powerful to give love and it is powerful to receive love. I learned this when I spent Thanksgiving with the Adams family.

Finally to the End of the Sayings of Rev. Shane

- The Christmas story begins with two ordinary people traveling 80 miles south from one insignificant town to another. God uses the ordinary!
- Mary and Joseph remind us that God reserves the right to alter the trajectory of the lives of ordinary people.
- Religion will try to change what you do but encountering Jesus will change who you are!
- I really don't like bad attitudes, bad churches or bad football...
- The good news: No surgery required on my broken finger. The bad news: My aspirations of being a hand model have been cruelly dashed.
- I would drink less Diet Coke if I lived in Greece. No ice or free refills...
- Our task in ministry today is to hold fast to our theology and be flexible with our methodology.
- Who is training young pastors to minister in a jumbotron and rock and roll band world?
- Absolutely wonderful day today! Can I get that in a 365 pack?
- Life is too short to live vicariously.
- Humans are hardwired in such a way that working together in unity of purpose produces exponential results.

- Many people treat prayer as if God were a cover band and we are making requests.
- The tough times in life provide us the opportunity to offer our most powerful witness to our faith!
- Faith is being able to trust that God's response to our prayers is the best response.
- Ben Franklin may be the most quoted of all Biblical authors.
- Too often in prayer we infer we are to keep asking until God hears us. In reality, we need to stay before God until we hear Him!
- Had lunch with Melissa and grandson Maddox, one of which kept sticking their hand into my soda.
- There is no Christian discipline more widely practiced and less generally understood than prayer.
- Church Oxymoron for the Day: Memorial Day Crowd
- Faithfulness does not mean that we conduct worship like they did in 1958; it means we live out our faith like they did in Acts 2.
- Got in three late night miles at the gym last night. Does this balance out the Buster Bar Blizzard I had after supper?
- Whiners believe people with good attitudes are just lucky.
- Whoever thought of putting BBQ sauce on a chicken burrito was a genius!

- Success, wealth and privilege are far greater temptations to the church than marginalization, poverty and persecution.
- Just because we can't do everything does not excuse us from doing something.
- Seminary trained me to minister in a bulletin, lectionary, piano and organ world. Not real helpful.
- Picked up my guitar the other day for the first time in a long time…felt like seeing an old friend with whom I no longer have anything in common.
- According to the Modified Rev. Shane Weight Watchers Scale, a medium DQ Blizzard is 1 point. A man on a 35-point system could eat 35 a day.
- You don't get to set your own Weight Watcher points.
- The hope of my salvation is not that I will from here forth be sinless, it is that God will forever be forgiving.
- I love preachers who can preach the paint off the walls. They get done and all that is left is sheet-rock. Paint is on the floor. Janitors have to vacuum it up.
- A great deal of what is classified as preaching is essentially baptized self-help material devoid of the power of the cross.

Smoky Mountain Trees
(Great Smoky Mountain National Park, circa 2006)

There is no place in the world Melissa and I like to visit more than the Tennessee side of the Great Smoky Mountains National Park. Her people come from that area (and I wish mine did) so we both have a real link to the land and the people. We have been there dozens of times and what we really love to do is day hike. We stay in really bad hotels (never stepping foot in Gatlinburg or Pigeon Forge), pack the SUV with iced Diet Pepsi, trail mix, Nature Valley Granola Bars and peanut butter and jelly sandwiches (we call trail steaks). Our adventures begin early as we find our selected trail head and set out for a day or part of a day. Melissa and I usually part company within a mile or two. She loves to push her body, get off the trail, forge ahead and work through the pain of walking straight up a mountain. She is almost always bleeding somewhere after a hike. While she is a character in "Lord of the Rings" desperately scaling Mt. Doom to dispose of the Ring of Power, I will sit at an overlook for half an hour eating a snack and thinking, *Is God like six kinds of awesome or what?!* Overlooking those blue, green mountains with their strands of mist hovering about them somehow fills my soul with peace.

What I like best are the trees. In the Smokies you can't really tell where one tree begins and another ends but the combined result is spectacular. Around our house in the Illinois suburbs of St. Louis we have some really great trees located in old subdivisions or cemeteries. They are majestic and perfect! You might infer that the canopy of the Great Smokies consists of similarly perfect trees all lined up in a row but you would have inferred wrongly. As we hike, I sometimes pass by some trees that have been pushed down by a storm and it always surprises me to see that none of them are perfect in any way. Where they enjoy sun exposure, they are well developed and gorgeous but parts of every tree are stunted and deformed where the sun could not reach them. As I walk, nature reminds me that each tree has, in its own way, paid a price to be a part of something greater than itself. I guess that is what being a part of a team is all about, sacrificing to be a part of something greater than ourselves.

A Slice of Life

Jesus found me in the spring of 1982. I was playing baseball for John A. Logan College and when I asked Jesus into my life, I got a good dose. I started a Christian music group called "El Shaddi." El Shaddi is a Hebrew name for God; we named our band "God." I started a Bible study for young people with my girlfriend Melissa (who later became my wife) and it seemed like half our town joined us. We loved Jesus so much and the fact we had no sense whatsoever made it all the better. When I transferred to Southern Illinois University at Carbondale, I shifted my evangelistic fervor to restroom walls. At SIU-C in the mid-80's, the restroom walls at Fahner Hall (where most History classes were held) were places of serious philosophical dialogue. People would offer a short treatise by writing it on the wall (Didn't Luther do this at Wittenberg?) and then future philosophers would offer rebuttal and comment. Thinking about how to be a witness for Jesus, I vandalized the restroom by writing on the wall, "Jesus Saves." Upon finishing my business, I looked forward to returning to see what impact my clear message had inflicted on the other history students. A couple of weeks later, I reentered the restroom to assess my evangelistic effectiveness. Right under my "Jesus Saves" someone had written, "And Gretsky scores on the rebound." Amen.

Christmas Lights
(Anywhere, USA circa timeless AD)

Have you noticed the wide variety of things people put in their yards to celebrate Christmas these days? Certainly the nativity-scape seems more cluttered than when only baby Jesus and Santa struggled for it just a generation ago. When our kids were growing up, we would sometimes drive around at night in mid-December and look at all the decorations. Some folks do nothing to celebrate; others tip their hat, some use good taste and some lose their minds in Clark Griswold or Tim the Tool Man fashion.

It was always the most high wattage, energy eating, gaudy and over-commercialized of efforts that got the ooh's and ah's from Zec and Lydia when they were small. There were always a few of these homes in the *lost their minds* category that grouped their décor into categorical clusters the way scientists classify animals and plants. Some had Disney characters in one quadrant, Fox network cartoon characters in another, Santa's entourage in one and a nativity in another. The nativity quadrant was often the oldest, most faded, least expensive and poorest lit. They normally consisted of three feet high, plastic figures of Mary and Joseph with a small light inside. These things weighed about six ounces, tended to tump over (is tump a word?) and on a windy night you could sometimes find Joseph rolling west down the street. (Mary never could get him to stay home.)

I always figured people bought their plastic, plug-in nativities before they franchised into secular markets; by the time we saw them, they clearly had lost some of their luster (and paint). I must confess that even my adult eyes are more quickly drawn to the wattage enhanced, blow-up Frosty the Snowman bobbing in the wind and churning up fake snow than the tiny Jesus tucked into the *circa* 1966 manger. I often wonder how people who don't know, would know, which one, was the One. Perhaps that is our problem these days at Christmas; we have trouble spotting Jesus in all the lights.

A Room in the Inn
(Fairview Heights, Illinois, circa 1997)

It was our first Christmas in Fairview Heights. Late
December 1997. We had run down to DuQuoin for a
holiday Friday/Saturday gift exchange with my mom and
dad. When we arrived at the parsonage late Saturday night,
it was clear something was wrong at 9 Keelan Drive. I left
the family in the car and cautiously unlocked the front door
of the house. As I slowly opened the door, a cold wind bit
my face. The frigid draft that assaulted me was from the
back sliding door which had been forcibly opened. It stood
wide open with the drapes dancing to the beat of a harsh
winter wind. The parsonage was ransacked. The thieves
had invaded our space, gone through our drawers and
cabinets, took what they wanted and worst of all...stolen our
Christmas gifts. I called the police and a couple of church
leaders.

The House of Bishop was shaken to the core. Would this
event define our entire Fairview Heights ministry? Would
fear enter my children and family? I felt lost in a strange
and faraway place. After the police arrived, a couple from
the church came by and extended an invitation to let us stay
the night with them. We jumped at the offer. It appears
there was room in the inn after all. I suppose we learned
something that night of Christmas. It was all about a young
family with nowhere to stay and about the grace in finding a
much-needed room for the night. It was about Christian
love and compassion lived out in a way that brings warmth
in a cold world. The next week Christmas gifts for the kids
began to pour in from the congregation; by the time

Christmas came around, we were no longer in an unfamiliar place surrounded by strangers…we were in our new home surrounded by family.

When my grandchildren are older, I will tell them this story right after I read the Christmas story from the Bible and before they open their presents. It will teach them that Christmas didn't just happen in Bethlehem some two thousand years ago...it is still happening today in the places our feet touch the ground!

- Encouragement to take personal responsibility for faith development is what people really need; it is seldom what they want.
- Character does not in and of itself make a great leader but you cannot be a great leader without it...
- Being a papa is good work if you can find it...
- Saw a church sign tonight that read, "DQ is not the only place with great Sundays." Who thinks of this stuff?
- Evangelism is a practical, not a conceptual thing. We need fewer books on the subject and more people just sharing Jesus!
- Technology and Church: What if Billy Graham had refused to be televised?
- Technology and Church: What if Martin Luther had issues with the printing press?
- Technology and Church: What if Paul had refused to travel on newfangled Roman roads?
- I have stopped being surprised when God does way cool things...
- Interesting how carols often define our Christmas ideas more than Scripture. Case in point: We Three Kings published in 1863.
- Did Herod the Great give himself that name?

- Anyone personally know any first century shepherds? I could stand to interview one or two.
- Is there such a thing as Thanksgiving eve where the Happy Puritan travels the world to bring the good children cans of cranberry sauce?
- Christian leaders today need a lung and a gill. A lung to minister to the old world. A gill to minister to the new.
- Why would we offer Christ anything other than our very best? I just don't get half-baked Christianity.
- Jesus said to pray for laborers for the harvest. He specifically asked us to do that. That is my prayer focus this week... Join me?
- Another softball game washed tonight; glad church is held in a stadium with a roof.
- "Jesus doesn't just want to tweet you. He wants to meet you." Why do I think this is really funny?
- What if churches thought less about spiritually feeding people and more about making them hungry?
- "God, I want to know you" is a far better prayer than, "God, let me tell you what you can do for me today."
- Rethink Mondays. New week. New opportunity. Carpe Diem my friend!
- Kittens are cool...just wait.
- Thinking about holiness devoid of legalism...seems like a winsome concept.
- If you don't give people some of what they want, you will never be in a position to give them any of what they need.

- Pre-preaching frozen coffee time happens at 7:45 a.m. each Sunday...the Apostle Peter also did this.
- Have never understood people's desire to be photographed holding a beer; it would be different were it a really difficult thing to do.
- It is inexcusable to allow someone to sit in church year after year and not directly challenge them to become a disciple of Jesus Christ.
- I spent my twenties trying to save the world through satire...didn't work.
- A lack of Biblical knowledge and understanding is a disease, but it is curable!
- There are two ways to live our Christian lives; we can live proactively or reactively. I would rather learn to throw hard than learn to duck quickly.
- When God is moving, it always gets the attention of those deeply invested in the status quo!
- Of all the gifts needed for long term ministry, the most essential is a short memory.
- Mourning is a type of prayer in which we painfully embrace our lack of control.
- God is crazy about us! For some of us this is an idea that will take some getting used to!

A Story about Jesus Turning Water into Teem
(*Somewhere in Arkansas, circa 1975*)

Growing up the child of a missionary/evangelist involved its share of uncertainty, but one thing remained constant throughout the years of my childhood; we came home for Christmas. There were years we couldn't afford many gifts, but we always arrived in Sunfield, Illinois, for the Christmas Eve program at the Methodist Church. After the program Santa would come out and I always wondered how he knew I was going to be there (being from out of state and all) but each year I received a gift.

One Christmas we were just barely able to afford the pilgrimage from Texas to Illinois. We stopped for lunch at a restaurant along the interstate called Tastee World, a companion to a Days Inn motel. We went in and intently gazed at the menu when Dad broke the news to us that we could not afford soft drinks. When dad ordered the pitcher of water, my face must have shown the horror of hearing those terrible words, but we had long since learned to make the best of things. When the waitress returned she said in a most chipper voice, "Here is your water," and poured it into our empty glasses. I picked up my glass, took a drink and my taste buds began to soar; powerfully, wonderfully, infinitely; it was TEEM! Teem, the lemon-lime soft drink complete with delicious bubbles and wondrous bouquet. A little later the waitress asked if we needed more water and returned with another pitcher of Teem. She winked at me with a compassionate smirk that revealed we had a little secret.

I don't remember what Santa gave me that year at Sunfield Methodist or what my parents got me for that matter, but I do remember the most wonderful gift ever received. A pitcher of Teem at a Tastee World restaurant from a waitress I didn't know in a town I don't remember. Perhaps baby Jesus on that special day turned the water into Teem just for a little boy going home for Christmas.

A Slice of Life

There were some famous doubters in the Bible. When
Abraham heard God was going to bless his ninety-year-old
wife Sarah with a son, he fell on his face and had a belly
laugh. God gave him a son anyway. When twelve spies
went into the Promised Land to get a report, ten of the spies
doubted they could drive out the Canaanites. Only Joshua
and Caleb entered the land. Luke tells us of a priest named
Zechariah who was told by an angel God was going to bless
his aged wife with a son. Zechariah doubted and God
rendered him unable to speak until John the Baptist was
born. I guess by the time He got to the New Testament,
God figured if you can't stop people from doubting, you
can at least keep them quiet.

Re-Conversion
(Sumner, Illinois, circa 1996)

Sometime in late 1992, I attended a seminar on how to do ministry with Senior Adults held in Peoria, Illinois. There was this feeble, little man who inched up to the platform (like Tim Conway used to do on the "Carol Burnet Show") and opened the thing up by proclaiming weakly, "God is Good." The people replied, "All the time" He quietly responded, "All the time" and they politely finished, "God is Good." I remember thinking to myself, "This is almost cool! I wonder what would happen if living people tried it?" The potential of this greeting captivated me and all I could think about was putting a V10 engine and glass packs on this thing and flooring it the very next week at Sumner. Our first four or five tries the next Sunday morning were a little lame but after that "God is good" became an institution. Every worship service I conducted at the Sumner United Methodist Church began with a rousing, "God is good!" It was a bold and upbeat way to begin our worship services...until that exceptionally cold winter.

It was Advent 1996. Advent in the United Methodist world is a traditional time of preparing our hearts for the arrival of the Christ Child on Christmas. On Wednesday, Melissa had been informed that our third child, a son we were to call Liam, had died in her womb. Nothing could be done until the next week and Sunday loomed in between. We were devastated. It was as if the best Christmas present in the world had been placed under the tree only to be snatched away in a cruel cosmic joke. Never had I felt so crushed, staggered and utterly...de-converted. All I could think about was the expectation that I would start the worship service with "God is Good!" I had no idea how I would do that. Never had I less perceived God to be good and the prospect of proclaiming it was more than my weary heart could bear.

These were the days before hospital privacy laws and everyone in our "One Casey's Town" (though we were yet to actually get a Casey's) knew what was happening. Rural folks know well how to dance with pain and death so they gave us space to hurt and when we walked into the church folks steered clear. On the bulletin were printed the name of Melissa Bishop followed by Shane Bishop. Melissa was scheduled to open by singing a song called "Harmony" with her best friend Sherri Baker about God's gift of a baby boy to creation. It seemed...ironic. I was to follow with a rousing, "God is good!" I could not possibly imagine how any of that was going to happen.

To my amazement, when the prelude concluded, Melissa (with our dead baby in her stomach) quietly arose from her seat and in beautiful harmony sang of a baby's arrival long ago. My stolid congregation listened with quivering lips, fighting back uncharacteristic tears as they marveled at the Spirit-energy of this incredible woman temporarily caught between a rock and a holy place. As I sat in awe of

Melissa's inner strength and the sheer power of her spirit, something occurred to me. If God is not good at this very minute; I mean "right now" then He wasn't good last week and wouldn't be good a month from now. It was as if God spoke to me, "I am either good or I am not good and you have about thirty seconds to decide." When the song ended, I walked behind that wooden pulpit and shouted for my soul, "God is Good!" to which the people nearly raised the roof as they replied, "All the Time!" I was re-converted. For the past two decades, I have opened each of our worship services with "God is Good" but never assume it is an easy thing. Sometimes you have to fight for it.

A Slice of Life

I often think about the occupation of Jesus' earthly father. The Greek text states that Joseph was a "tekton," an artisan who made things of wood, stone or metal. I am thinking he worked with stone...nativity sets mainly.

A Final Story
(Fairview Heights, Illinois, circa 2012)

As I write this, today is our wedding anniversary. On May 21, 1983 Melissa Anne Martin and Shane Lavern Bishop (we have already discussed the middle name) were united in holy matrimony at the First Baptist Church in DuQuoin, Illinois. I truly don't know what we were thinking. I was between my junior and senior year of college at Southern Illinois University-Carbondale and would spend my final semester student teaching before graduation. It would be a year before I could even seek gainful employment. Melissa was babysitting for a whopping $60 a week. After our tithe, that left $54 whether we needed it or not. Our plan was to move into the tiny house trailer my grandma had lived in before she died (having hoarded hundreds of containers of dental floss), hang on for a year, find me a teaching/coaching job and get out of town. They tell me a lot of folks were really surprised we threw our lot in together and didn't think it would last, that we were too different. It appears they were wrong.

Last Saturday, Zec and Sarah and Ryan and Lydia found babysitters for the kids and we took them to Andria's Steakhouse to celebrate. There are a lot of fancy restaurants in St. Louis, but I don't understand what they are trying to do and I don't like the food. They give you tiny portions of yucky stuff that you are supposed to like because it was expensive. I don't get it. I get Andria's. They have a menu I understand and serve the very best beef tenderloin filets on the planet. Andria's is our special occasion place and we had plenty to celebrate! Zec just got promoted, Sarah is expecting grandchild number four (I have suggested Delmar for a name regardless of whether it is a boy or a girl), Lydia finished a 4.0 college semester and Ryan was voted high school Tennis Coach of the Year on both the girls and boys side in our region. We are blessed beyond anything I could have ever imagined for a 165-pound groom in a black and white tuxedo and a mullet.

As is usual in such family situations, I didn't talk much (I have to talk all the time at work) as the conversation lightly bounced between careers, children, church and marriage. I didn't really keep up with the conversation as well as I should have because I was really busy…being grateful. I kept thinking about all those times when I put church ahead of my marriage and family, when I was pushing eighty-hour work weeks and it would have been so easy for Melissa to take the kids, walk out the door and never look back, but she didn't; she wanted to but she didn't. She stayed with me! She said she would stay with me in that Baptist Church in 1983 and she has stayed with me. She believed God had a special calling on my life and she wasn't about to let me blow it. She believed God was going to give her the family she never had and she was willing to fight for it. She believed that blessing waited on the other side of pain and she wasn't going to miss it. Melissa is a fighter. Melissa is my hero.

Life is good. Almost every day I get to spend time with my grandchildren. Being a Papa has turned out to be one of the few things in my life that wasn't overrated. Maddox Bishop Blaha is about to turn three; he is blessed with perpetual energy, looks like his Papa and thinks I am the "greatest hero in the world." Elijah Christian Bishop just turned two and I call him the "name bearer." He is more reserved than Maddox but like me, thinks he is hilarious. He will never have trouble entertaining himself. His father Zec must have liked his middle name better than I liked mine, so the House of Bishop is now working our second generation of "Christians" after three generations of "Lavern(e)s." I hope ABC does not come out with a show next year about two single women working in a Milwaukee brewery called "Laverne and Christian." That would set us back five generations. Eli will take the name of Bishop that my dad passed down to me and carry it into the future. It is a heavy responsibility to be trusted with a good name. And then there is Mabry McKenna Blaha. She just turned one and holds her own just fine. She really likes our Golden Retriever Mia and we are all crazy about her. She smiles every time she sees me and will bite your finger in two if it gets too close to any of her six teeth. As if that weren't enough, my mom and dad moved to the area a couple of years ago; I cherish my time with them. Dad and I walk almost every morning and grab a quick breakfast before work. My big time with mom is Sunday after church when we go to lunch. Mom held our family together when I was a kid and now she relishes her role at Christ Church she calls "Senior Pastor's Mom." (We may have to get her an office.) In addition, I am more in love with Melissa than I have ever been in my life and enjoy every moment we spend together. Our long Jeep rides and Smoky Mountain adventures don't come around as often since the grandkids arrived but we are happy and fulfilled.

Twenty-nine years to be married to one person is a long time. Not all the years were great and some were not even good. I don't know that there are any perfect marriages. I don't know that God has that "one special person" for everyone but I am sure of this; had Melissa and I not stuck it out in the hard times, there would have been nothing to celebrate on this night.

About the Author
Shane L. Bishop

Rev. Shane Bishop has been the Senior Pastor at Christ Church in Fairview Heights, Illinois, since 1997. In 2010 Shane was named a Distinguished Evangelist of the United Methodist Church by the Foundation for Evangelism. With his strengths of vision casting, preaching and leadership, weekend worship attendance has increased from approximately 200 in 1996 to 1,700. The Illinois Great River Annual Conference has recognized Christ Church six times with the Award for Church Growth and Evangelism.

A former history teacher and coach, Shane holds both graduate and undergraduate degrees from Southern Illinois University-Carbondale. An Elder in the Illinois Great Rivers Conference, Shane graduated cum laude in 1992 from Candler School of Theology at Emory University. There he received the Rollins Scholarship Award for his strong academic work and effectiveness in pastoral leadership at the St. James-Manchester Charge in Manchester, Georgia. From 1992-1997 he served the rural Sumner/Beulah Charge in Sumner, Illinois where he was presented the Denman Evangelism Award in 1994 before being appointed to Christ United Methodist Church in 1997.

Elected to represent the Illinois Great Rivers Conference (IGRC) at General Conference three times and Jurisdictional Conference four times, Shane has traveled extensively around the country and the world. Christ Church has partnered to charter sister congregations in both the Philippines and Honduras. They have also planted two regional campuses.

Shane resides in Belleville, Illinois, with his wife Melissa. The couple has two married children and four grandchildren. He enjoys hiking the Smoky Mountains, playing NSA Softball, American History and the St. Louis Cardinals.